The Prevention of Money Laundering and Terrorist Financing

keeping the hurdles High!

John Howell

Illustrations by David Langdon

Official Typologies from FATF

ICC Commercial Crime Services

First published in 2006 by
ICC Commercial Crime Services
Maritime House
1 Linton Road
Barking
Essex IG11 8HG
www.icc-ccs.org

ICC Publication 669

A catalogue record for this book is available from the British Library.

ISBN-10: 92-842-0002-4
ISBN-13: 978-92-842-0002-3

Drawings by David Langdon
Design & Typesetting: Devdan Sen
Cover Photograph: © istockphoto.com/Michael Ledray
Printed in Cranleigh, England by Entaprint

CONTENTS

FOREWORD

Nothing is more important to the International Chamber of Commerce (ICC) than the physical and economic safety of markets and their participants. Our objective is to inform and motivate the ICC's stakeholder base at large – the staff and customers of member companies and associations, as well as the professional service providers who support them.

Recent changes in anti-money laundering and anti-terrorist finance legislation means that these very people are now the so-called "gatekeepers" of the financial system. They are no longer to be found just in financial institutions, but in all walks of life and in countries at all stages of development. They are our front line of defence against organised crime and terrorist groups.

Without the proper training, and in the absence of support and understanding from all concerned, the task of gatekeepers becomes impossible. Both they and the global community they serve are at risk. Conversely, the combination of a well-motivated and trained workforce with an understanding and supportive clientele create a highly hostile environment for those bent on manipulating financial systems.

We know this from our long commitment to fighting corruption, money laundering and terrorist financing. The ICC Commercial Crime Services is the commercial crime arm of the ICC and has played a key role in the prevention and control of fraud and money laundering. They are the co-producers of this book.

The ICC provides input through its national committees in countries around the world on decisions that crucially affect corporate strategies and the bottom line. It works with national governments, international organisations and the UN to strengthen links between business and governments, contributing towards a secure world business environment. In particular, the ICC works closely with the G8 and is thus honoured to support the Financial Action Task Force (FATF) process and grateful to them for their help in developing this resource.

This book is essential reading for corporations, their staff and customers. Law enforcement agencies may also find it useful, especially as insight into the challenges faced by businesses. It forms part of the ICC's wider contribution to protecting the integrity of the global market and its participants against criminal and terrorist threats.

Guy Sebban

Secretary General
International Chamber of Commerce

PREFACE TO THE INTERNATIONAL EDITION

An ever-wider range of money laundering and terrorist financing laws are being introduced to protect the innocent and pursue the guilty. At some stage in their career, everyone who engages in business, as buyer or seller, will be affected by them, for example by joining a firm subject to money laundering regulations, or by being a client subject to client identification rules.

In responding to money laundering and terrorist financing, mutual self-protection by the many has become equally important, if not more so, than specialist protection by the few. The weighty and often expensive specialist guides on these subjects (there are over 150 on the UK books in print list alone) do not easily meet the needs of the many.

This completely new International Chamber of Commerce (ICC) Guide thus aims to support the far wider audience who are now the front line of defence against organised crime and terrorism – those with day-to-day dealings with the public in business and law enforcement. It is also for those who require an introduction or reintroduction to the subject as a basis for more detailed study.

Above all the book provides a straightforward and user-friendly path to knowledge and general skills that, all too often, have been portrayed as too complex for the average person. In fact, for the many millions now subject to regulations, self protection now necessarily relies on a high degree of applied common sense.

The international edition has been written to be universally applicable and presents a composite picture of standards for anti-money laundering and anti-terrorist finance regimes to be found globally. This is to help readers understand the basic problems, threats and regulatory frameworks common to all countries and how to respond appropriately. Where there is demand, specific national editions will follow.

I am most grateful to the Financial Action Task Force (FATF) for permission to reproduce their official typologies case reports to illustrate the points made in the text. These examples are important because they show money laundering for the mundane activity it so very often seems to be. Such cases have also played a role in informing policymaking and thus help the reader to gain an insight into why policy has been framed in a given way. The appendices contain references to further sources of help, including on-line research resources.

Many people have helped with this Guide. Sarah Richards helped with the first drafts and the final text has greatly benefited from a detailed reading by David Hughes (Berwin Leighton Paisner). Thanks are also due to Fred Horbeek (formerly of Rabobank) Andreas Pavelka (Credit Suisse) and Guy Scammell (formerly of RBC) for the Peer Review. Cecille Goddard (Jordans), Julian Philips (JP Risk) and Ian Trumper (Forensic Accounting) provided invaluable specialist input along the way.

I would like to thank my colleagues Prof. Henk Elffers (NICR/Antwerp), Prof. Mike Levi (Cardiff), Prof. David Llewellyn (Loughborough) and Prof. Piet van Reenen (Utrecht) for their loyalty and friendship, likewise the Management Board and staff of the State Bank of Baden-Württemberg (L-Bank) for a decade of unwavering support.

This initiative would, of course, have been impossible without the encouragement of Capt. Pottengal Mukundan and the team at ICC – CCS.

Finally, a picture (so we are told) is worth a thousand words. We were privileged to have David Langdon agree to provide the illustrations, strictly for cash, of course...

John Howell
jh@compliance.u-net.com

February 2006

ONE

What is Money Laundering?

Traditional Definitions

Money Laundering

Put simply, money laundering is the process of making criminal assets appear legitimate. It is important to note that these assets are not just:

- money—they can be anything of value
- *proceeds* of crime—they can be assets intended for use in future crime (sometimes humorously called the *"precedes" of* crime).

The scope of activities that constitute money laundering is now quite wide, both in law and in practice. A good starting point for getting to grips with such a wide subject is the frequently used traditional description of how criminal cash assets are laundered. This is defined as a three-stage cycle comprising three distinct processes—*placement, layering and integration.*

Placement describes how cash, such as the small denomination notes typically generated by drugs trafficking, are quickly dispersed away from the scene of crime and placed in the financial system. Beforehand, the cash may pass through a series of businesses that trade on a cash basis, such as shops or restaurants. This is to mix up the amounts involved and otherwise disguise its distinguishing characteristics. The cash is then banked in amounts designed to avoid cash deposit or suspicious activity report filing requirements, a process known in some instances as "smurfing".

The illicit nature of the assets can then be hidden further by the process of *layering.* This basically involves repeated banking and commercial transactions designed to make the real origin of the assets as hard as possible to identify and to prevent the construction of an audit trail leading back to the proceeds of the original crime and its perpetrators.

The final stage is *integration,* when laundered assets from one or more crimes are collected ready for open use. Well integrated into the system, they have all the appearance of legitimate funds and need not be laundered further.

The Money Laundering Learning Curve

Unfortunately, reality is never as simple as text book descriptions. It is hard sometimes to work out where one stage begins and another ends. Some stages may be combined by money launderers if it is safe to do so. You may hear these expressions used loosely to describe what is in fact part (or all) of a money laundering process. Nonetheless, the three stages are a useful way of understanding the "big picture" of what goes on, not only with cash, but also with other forms of proceeds.

Terrorist Financing

A useful distinction that can be made about money used to fund terrorism is between:

- terrorist funding—basically the collection of funds for use by terrorist groups
- terrorist financing—used to describe the movement of money needed by terrorists to undertake specific operations.

The initial activities of terrorist funding may not fit into the classical money laundering model. For example, the funds may be collected very openly and legally via a humanitarian or cultural association.

The point at which they are diverted from legitimate fund-raising channels towards terrorist activity, and thus the point where terrorist funding begins, can be hard to distinguish.

Similarly, it can be very hard to distinguish when overseas use of a credit or debit card is a legitimate means of remitting funds and when it is terrorist financing, e.g. where the money is later used to feed and house a group of suicide bombers pending a terrorist attack.

Self-Laundering

In some countries courts take the view that you don't need to use other people to launder money. Criminals who keep the proceeds of crime in their own bank account can be guilty of so-called "self-laundering". The same applies to assets arising from tax evasion—a sobering thought for many, as penalties for money laundering can be much higher than those for tax evasion

In all Cases, Caution and common Sense

Taking all these points together you might say that the term "money laundering" covers the:

- way criminals store, move and convert their resources around the world, and
- methods they use to disguise and conceal these operations

- thought processes involved

These points apply to both money laundering in the traditional sense as well as to the movement of money for terrorism. The term "money laundering" is therefore used in this book to cover both threats, with distinctions made as necessary.

Realising that words are used loosely, and can thus cause confusion, helps an understanding of the key point about successful prevention of money laundering and terrorist financing—the need for caution and common sense. What is in a name or description is not so important as *who* or *what* is behind a person or a transaction.

FATF Example 1: Prepaid international telephone cards serve as a cover for money laundering

Two banks in a European country (Country C) filed a series of Suspicions Activity Report (SARs) related to unusual deposits of cash made by the director of a domestic limited company involved in the trade of prepaid international telephonic cards in Country C and an African country (Country D). The cash funds, credited at regular intervals of time also by means of the manager's relatives, were periodically transferred to a small company registered in another country (Country E), which was supposed to be the seller of the relevant telephone cards.

From research carried out by the Financial Intelligence Unit (FIU) in Country C, the Country E registered company seemed to be a shell company without any real economic activity. On this premise, in order to investigate further in the matter, the FIU contacted the FIU in Country E. Thanks to the co-operation between the two FIUs it has been disclosed that the:

- competent authorities in Country E were already conducting an independent investigation of the Country E company for suspicious financial transactions .
- nature of shell company of the company could be confirmed.
- Country D partner of the Country C company was under investigation by the Country E customs authority for narcotics trafficking.

The History and Scope of the Problem

Many of the activities that now constitute the criminal offence of money laundering have a long tradition and still occur widely. Money laundering is not a crime restricted just to emerging economies or to countries where law enforcement lacks resources. The financial capitals of the world's richest nations have all had large-scale money laundering scandals in the recent past.

Tip of a dangerous Iceberg

Though it has not always been tackled as vigorously as it is now, historically money laundering was never a minor issue. It was always known to be associated with serious crime, especially large scale racketeering in drink, prostitution, shady businesses and corrupt public institutions.

However, unlike handling stolen goods (a capital offence in many countries until the 19th century) money laundering did not attract the direct attention of law enforcement authorities in a concerted way internationally until well into the 20th century. In the 1960's and 70's technology, new political power structures and a booming international economy greatly facilitated money laundering.

In the early 20th century it was mostly local, and sometimes national, criminals who laundered the proceeds of crime through Mafia-style organisations, typified by Al Capone and his gang. A law unto themselves, they relied on violence and frequently murder to ensure co-operation with, and stifle opposition to, their schemes. This tradition of violence lives on today in some countries.

In the second half of the 20th century money laundering increased in scale, the main drivers being drugs, corruption, organised crime, fraud, terrorism and civil war.

Drugs

This includes the production, transport and sale of illegal drugs, especially heroin and cocaine, from the Middle East, Asia and South America to North America and Europe. Latterly the production of so-called "designer drugs" in Europe and Asia has joined this list.

In its 2005 World Drug Report, the UN estimates that "5% of the world's global population age 15-64...consumed illicit drugs at least once in the last 12 months". It estimates the retail value of the world drug trade at US$ 321bn. These proceeds have to be laundered by the various participants of the drug supply chain; the producers, the wholesalers, the retailers and the individual pushers.

FATF Example 2: Cash narcotics proceeds smuggled to a free trade zone

In one narcotics consuming country (Country B), bags of money which were the product of illegal drug sales, in amounts of approximately US$ 700,000 weekly, were handed over to two individuals. The total amount involved is estimated to have been USD 13 million. The money was given by the individuals to jewellery stores in the city where the illegal proceeds had been generated. The stores in turn deposited the funds into various banks in amounts just under the SAR reporting threshold. With the funds from the deposits, the jewellery stores bought cheques whose beneficiary was a firm that belonged to one of the individuals in the free trade zone (FTZ) of a nearby country (Country C).

In the FTZ, the cheques were used by the firm to pay for imports from an important narcotics producing country (Country D), and a commission was obtained for this service. Also, importers from Country D settled their export transactions by making payments to the enterprises indicated by the second individual. The cheques were deposited by various companies located of the FTZ into banks located within the zone, as payment for real and legitimate purchases from importers from Country B.

One of the individuals was prosecuted and convicted in Country B for money laundering, with a reduced sentence for having co-operated with the authorities. The second individual was convicted for money laundering in Country C. The FTZ business that had been used in the operation was closed by the authorities and the physical goods that it contained were confiscated by the Government. There was no charge made against banks.

Corruption

The second half of the 20th century also saw the birth of many new countries following de-colonisation. Independence was not always easy and old colonial powers have continued to support their former territories with grants in aid. Likewise superpowers supported long-established but failing states as part of the Cold War.

Corrupt politicians, officials and their associates used their positions to defraud their countries of these aid monies as well as natural assets and tax income, in addition to taking bribes for political favours.

The proceeds of theft and corruption were then laundered to bank accounts abroad. There are countries in almost every continent where privileged persons have illegally exported state assets offshore for themselves and their families. In some countries they continue to do so.

Such corruption often involves senior officials turning a blind eye to criminal activity in, or based in, a given country. Some countries' economies run on the laundered proceeds of national and international crime. The value of these flows over the past decade has amounted to many billions of dollars.

FATF Example 3: Laundering the proceeds of embezzlement

The bank accounts of a petroleum minister (Mr. Y) of a former dictatorship under which numerous embezzlement offences had been committed were credited with a sum of USD 6 million in the space of a few months. This provided grounds for the case to be referred to the judicial authorities who decided to indict the minister.

On investigation the FIU discovered that Mr. Y was operating under the cover of an alias. The recently opened account controlled by Mr. Y had been credited with a notary's cheque for over USD 575,000 corresponding to the sale of a property. This sum did not correspond in any way to the market value of the property.

Organised Crime

As well as complex, high value robbery, organised crime lies behind kidnapping, blackmail, murder and contract killing, prostitution and child pornography, as well as the smuggling of illegally obtained natural resources, weapons, people, alcohol, and tobacco. Wherever laws limit the availability or price of goods or services, organised crime will try to fill the gap in the market.

FATF Example 4: Laundering the proceeds of Human Smuggling
The Slovenian FIU has worked on a case which involved a Slovenian citizen, who was the leading member of an organised criminal association dealing with smuggling of illegal refugees, mostly Turkish, Albanian, Macedonian and Iranian citizens, to the West. In the years 1998 to 2003, this Slovenian citizen received 81 money orders from 14 different individuals from the USA, 'the former Yugoslav Republic of Macedonia", Italy and Germany for a total amount of 40,000,000 Slovene tolars. In connection with this transaction, the FIU had reason to believe that the money derived from the organisation of illegal migration or from the participation of the suspect in the group for the organisation of illegal migration. The biggest share of money was remitted to Slovenia from the USA in the amount of 31,000,000 Slovene tolars or 77% of all money orders in the amount of 40,000,000 Slovene tolars. The main portion of this money remained in Slovenia and was thought to be used for investment into real estate and was also distributed among other members of the criminal association. In the year 2000 the suspect's wife, who has not filed an income tax statement for that year, used 14,000,000 Slovene tolars to buy real estate. The FIU also found out that both the suspect and his wife had made transactions representing several times their official income (as filed in their income tax statements during the years 1998 to 2003). The suspect was finally convicted in 2003, in connection with the amount of 40,000,000 Slovene tolars, for organisation of illegal migration.

Fraud
In some cases a business may be "merely" the unwitting conduit of money laundering. Too often, however, it is also the victim, with the offence giving rise to the money laundering being a fraud on its own,

or its customers' or its creditors' funds. It may also be victim of a fraud because an "honest employee" is in fact an infiltrator from a criminal gang. It may have entered into fictitious business as part of an elaborate sting against it.

FATF Example 5: Cash criminal proceeds placed in the financial system through margin trading

This case involved the theft of some USD 384 million from a bank in Country T over the ten-year period from 1992 to 2001. The money was sent to Country G and laundered through a serious of companies and accounts (to date 80 companies and 550 bank accounts are involved, but this is growing as the investigation progresses). Much of the money was invested in the property and stock markets in Country G and ultimately used at will by the four principal thieves for whatever they wanted. At one time in the mid-nineties one of the thieves was reported as being the largest margin stock investor in the Country G market. There was a huge turnover in stocks and shares through some of Country G companies, as well as dividends from shares held long term. The true extent of the dealing is only just coming to light but it is evident that the majority of the funds stolen in Country T occurred after 1997 when a regional economic downturn adversely affected the local property and stock markets. It is of interest that no disclosures were ever made by stockbrokers about the dealings of these companies. At this time four people have been charged with money laundering and have been released on bail, and a number of other people are fugitives.

Terrorism and War

Money laundering also facilitates terrorist campaigns, civil wars and genocide associated with the late 20th and early 21st centuries. To fund armed conflict, militants run "front" companies that are easy to set up, such as taxi, laundry and waste disposal businesses. They use these companies both to generate revenue and to channel the proceeds of crime into war-chests. Some groups also channel funds through humanitarian organisations, which they set up or take control of for that purpose.

Recent civil wars in Africa and Asia have been financed partly by the sale of scarce natural resources, such as gems (so-called "blood diamonds"), minerals (cobalt) and wood, from the territories they control or capture. In some cases they take over whole sections of the economy and launder the proceeds overseas to buy arms.

FATF Example 6: Diamond trading allegedly finances terrorist organisation

This case consists of two parts. Its common denominator is traffic in precious stones. The starting point was a transaction in diamonds to finance an Islamic terrorist organisation. A diamond dealer from a Middle Eastern country, but established in Europe, seems to have been used as an intermediary to sell diamonds bought at market prices in a west African country and shipped through a neighbouring African country. The profits on this transaction were apparently used to fund Osama Ben Laden's Al Qaïda organisation.

The person concerned is on a list of 135 persons forbidden to travel under UN Security Council Resolution 1343 (2001) because of his involvement in diamond trafficking in favour of a revolutionary movement in Sierra Leone. Some years ago, he reportedly participated in a series of terrorist attacks in Africa.

Moreover, this individual and his family seem to have relations with another family of diamond dealers—with the same origins—whose bank account movements may conceal a particularly interesting money laundering mechanism.

The parties involved in this second part took a loan of about USD 3.8 million with a bank in Country T. It was not so much the use of these funds which raised a problem (as their origin was not under a cloud) as the debt repayment terms, which could allow the borrowers to repay their loan by laundering the proceeds from crime, probably diamond trafficking. Moreover, before the funds were transferred for payment in Country T, they had probably already been pre-laundered through intermediate banks in different European countries.

The events in the USA of 11th September 2001 also brought home the vulnerability of open societies to terrorist attacks. Terrorist organisations have been shown to operate internationally with relative ease, deadly local effect and with even deadlier wider repercussions.

Not victimless Offences

Whilst money laundering may seem relatively harmless it enables some of the most harmful criminal activities that exist. The following table shows the types of crimes (known as "precursor offences") that by international agreement give rise automatically to money laundering offences. They are far from being "victimless" crimes.

Types of offences giving rise to money laundering offences:

- Organised crime and racketeering
- Terrorism and terrorist financing
- Sexual exploitation especially of children
- Trafficking (drugs, arms, people) and smuggling
- Corruption and bribery
- Fraud
- Counterfeiting (currency / goods) and forgery
- Environmental crime
- Murder and grievous bodily harm
- Robbery or theft
- Extortion
- Piracy
- Insider trading and market manipulation

Source: FATF 40 Recommendations June 2003

Because of the actual and potential damage money laundering can cause, a number of countries have taken a bolder approach and said that all crimes, or crimes above a certain penalty threshold, are precursor offences.

Tackling Crime by tackling Money Laundering

It is very hard for law enforcers to investigate crimes on a day-to-day basis let alone to try to prevent them. By making it hard to undertake criminal operations in the first place and hard to profit from them, the fight against money laundering is above all an attempt to prevent future crime with all its disruptive, costly and other negative consequences for society.

Accordingly, most countries have a strict legal framework against money laundering. But even where nationals of a country respect the law, the low risk of detection or sanction may encourage foreign criminals and terrorists to set up operations in that country and use its banks and businesses for money laundering purposes.

Different countries face different scales of money laundering risk, and risks may vary between business sectors in one particular country. Also, just as business is always on the move and looking for new opportunities, so unfortunately, are money launderers. Risks can change overnight and businesses are even more exposed where official responses are weak because of other threats or low resources.

Using this book and the other resources mentioned in Appendix 2 you can put in place your first line of defence yourself, and reduce the risk of becoming a victim of money laundering. Unfortunately, one of the ways of becoming a victim is negligently or recklessly becoming involved in money laundering schemes or turning a blind eye to them—the savings in time and financial incentives may make this seem an attractive proposition or a path of least resistance.

For those who consider anti-money laundering (or "AML") precautions optional, a word of warning: By international agreement penalties for involvement in money laundering have been set with an eye on deterring such thoughts. In the UK the most serious money laundering offences attract a maximum prison sentence of fourteen years, and other countries are equally, if not more, strict.

TWO

Who?, How? and Why?

How is Money Laundered?

As every legal transaction is a potential cover for an illegal one, there are, in theory, any number of ways to launder money. However, by going back to basics again—money laundering defined as storing, moving and converting assets—and by seeing it as making illegal transactions look like legal ones, some useful common threads emerge.

Direct Access to the banking System

Laundering cash usually involves attempts to make use of banking systems. Because they offer the easiest way to deposit, transfer and pay out money, banks also offer the simplest way of storing, moving and converting cash assets nationally and internationally. The world's powerful financial institutions can have cash or liquid financial instruments (such as bonds and shares) purchased, converted and transferred in and out of most countries and currencies within 24 hours by electronic payment systems (often called "wires" or "wire transfers").

The ideal form of access from the criminals' point of view is to trick a financial institution into accepting them as *bona fide* clients and their cash and other financial instruments as *bona fide* assets. They can then give their own instructions to deposit and transfer cash and financial instruments around the world and use everyday means, such as bank cards, credit cards, cheques and giros, to control the flows.

Because some countries are thought to be less strict on money laundering, laundering can also involve moving cash between countries, taking advantage of lax or non-existent controls on cross border currency movements to place money in foreign banking systems. Cash smuggling is a big problem, and not just in areas of the world where the informal economy is strong.

Indirect Access to the banking System

Indirect access to the same facilities can be gained when money launderers trick businesses and individuals to act as a "backdoor" route into the banking system. Unlike financial institutions, in some countries, lawyers, accountants, independent financial advisers and dealers in high value goods can still establish or maintain ongoing business relationships with people they scarcely know. They can then:

Backdoor banking

- accept large payments in cash—even on a continual basis
- pay third parties for goods and services received by a customer (e.g. by their own cheque paid to the customer's order)
- operate bank accounts for clients, e.g. under a power of attorney or by book entry in their client funds accounts.

Once the business relationship is established, such professionals unwittingly allow launderers to make deposits, transfers and payments by "remote control" through them, using arrangements really intended for *bona fide* clients.

Alternative Remittance Systems (ARS)

Not everyone has access to a bank account and not every country in the world has an efficient and effective banking system. Specialised money remittance companies and alternative remittance systems established by other types of companies and individuals also offer services that enable money to be deposited in one country or area and collected in another, either by the depositor or someone nominated by them. Electronic funds transfer by fax and e-mail is also possible via such systems.

Till recently, ARS were usually unregulated and open to abuse by money launderers. They are now increasingly regulated but sometimes still offer an alternative way of moving, sorting and converting value whilst avoiding more regulated areas (see Chapter 7 for more on this topic).

FATF Example 7: Wire transfers are used as part of a terrorist fund-raising campaign

An investigation in Country A of Company Z, a company thought to be involved in the smuggling and distribution of pseudoephedrine (a suspected source of revenue for terrorist organisations), revealed that employees of Company Z were sending a large number of negotiable cheques to Country B. Additional evidence revealed that the target business was acting as an unlicensed money remitter. Based on the above information, search warrants were obtained for the Company Z premises and two residences. Analysis of the documents and bank records seized as a result of the search warrants indicated that the suspects had wire transferred money to an individual with suspected ties to a terrorist group.

Physical Alternatives to financial Instruments

If money-launderers cannot get their assets into a banking system, then they must be kept in physical form. This can involve holding financial assets (such as cash, travellers' cheques, and bearer stocks and shares) or in items that can easily be converted to cash (such as cars, watches, jewellery, precious metals and stones, antiques or works of art).

These assets are then stored or passed around according to where they are needed and where it is safe to move and convert them. Some of the physical forms of asset have the advantage of being easier to smuggle between countries.

FATF Example 8: Criminal attempts to launder fraud proceeds through the diamond market

A known criminal who had benefited financially from a fraud that took place outside Country A attempted to send money to jewellers. This was with a view to purchasing precious stones. The financial institution holding the account had been concerned about the individual for some time and had made several suspicious transaction reports to the FIU in Country A. The client attempted to send USD 8.2 million to the jewellers. Before this took place the bank took the commercial decision to freeze the accounts. The law enforcement agency made initial investigations and was satisfied that the attempt to buy precious stones had been an attempt to launder the proceeds of the fraud.

Complex Schemes

To be able to use the channels described above, money launderers must have means of making and accepting payments. Like any other businessmen they have a choice of building, buying or borrowing channels.

Setting up a company not only provides a business activity to hide behind, but also offers anonymity and respectability. Criminal transactions are hidden in ordinary trade, and only a few employees may be party to what is really going on. A company can be purchased for this purpose and simply abandoned to its fate when its usefulness has passed.

Another way is for launderers to get one of their members inside an established business and "borrow" its banking facilities, passing money-laundering transactions though the company's books. It may take some imaginative accounting but it can be done—and is.

Again, with so many possibilities, it is impossible to describe all the forms money laundering can take. However, set out in the subsequent chapters are outlines of how specific types of business are at risk and examples of past money laundering schemes.

FATF Example 9: Market manipulation of company stock launders funds and produces added profit

The money in question came from a drug-trafficking organisation and was used to purchase two listed companies. During an investigation by the police of Country V into the laundering of money from drug trafficking, it was found that a money launderer had planned and executed a plan to feed large sums of money from a mafia-related organisation into the stock market. The money, which was the proceeds of various frauds, was deposited in a private bank, controlled by the mafia organisation itself, located in Country R located in the Caribbean region.

The plan included the purchase of two companies established in Country V and listed on the stock market. These were a stock brokerage and a small bank. The first stage took place as planned. Numerous small investors from abroad using false names bought the shares in the two firms. The aim was to ensure that none of the investors bought more than the percentage of ownership that would have required reporting under country V's laws.

Through fictitious general shareholders' meetings in which lawyers were involved, a new board of directors was appointed with people acting as front men for the money launderer, Mr. W. Upon gaining control of the two companies, Mr. W immediately granted full powers to the members of the criminal organisation, thus guaranteeing their control over the money.

Subsequently a share increase was applied for, and all the legal requirements were met. Again, they took care to ensure none of the investors exceeded the 5 percent limit. The share increase in the two companies came to approximately USD 42 million, which was subscribed and disbursed through banks in Country V. In reality the proceeds of the market manipulation, including the original funds, were then laundered by transferring the money from Country R to banks in Europe, from where it was transferred to Company N was located in Country Y, another offshore financial centre, which owned marble mines in South America. The money then returned to Country R, having first passed through accounts in Europe and North America. The same money then went around the circuit again, so as to simulate foreign investments in the share capital of the two companies.

Through this circular process of share buying and selling the price of the shares rose to 640 percent of their face value. To achieve this, the complicity of the brokers trading in the shares on the stock market

Using a "False Front" company to disguise reality

was necessary. The over-priced shares were subsequently delivered to the Mafia investors who were the final victims of the fraud when the police prevented the money launderer from controlling the price of the shares.

Who are the Launderers?

Launderers use many identities—even their real name if it is safe to do so. But mostly they pay, force or trick people to work for them, or operate through companies, charities, or finance houses that look like normal organisations ("false fronts").

By channelling transactions through company after company, person after person, bank after bank especially in countries where money-laundering controls are weak, they build up a strong cover. By the time the cover is penetrated (if at all), the launderers are usually long gone.

Again, this is designed to make sure the assets involved cannot be traced back to them or any organisation involved.

Individuals and petty Criminals

As most crime can give rise to money laundering, most criminals are money launderers, one way or another. At the lower end of the scale is the thief who, for example, borrows money from an unlicensed moneylender (or "Loan Shark") to bribe a guard whilst some machinery is stolen.

The "shark" advances money without asking too many questions about its intended use—at a price. Once the crime has been committed the thief will need to repay the Shark. He sells the stolen machinery to a "Fence" or person who deals in stolen goods. The price he gets will not reflect the true value of the machinery, but again, there will be no questions asked.

What the Thief, Loan Shark and the Fence do not realise is that, in addition to any other crime they may have committed, they have

"Beware the Loan Shark, my son…"

probably committed a money laundering offence. Moreover, it may carry a stiffer penalty than theft, accessory to theft or handing stolen goods.

Professional Gangs

More complex crimes, and crimes involving larger sums, require more complex laundering arrangements. In these cases launderers are usually part of a criminal organisation that specialises in laundering other criminals' money. They may be, or act as introducers to, corrupt professionals (e.g. lawyers, accountants or bankers) who take a payment to set up a money-laundering scheme in support of a particular criminal operation.

In such cases, money laundering is organised along business lines, and is often international in scope. Whether individuals, local gangs, organised national or international groups are involved, the motivation is first and foremost money. However, not all money laundering is motivated by greed alone.

Terrorist Funding

Throughout the world, there is a minority of political activists the members of which are prepared to use sudden and indiscriminate attacks on people and property to attain their objectives. To some they may be heroes or freedom fighters. Under international law they are terrorists, and those who help them are supporters of terrorism.

The range of causes linked to terrorist activity is wider than many people think. It includes environmental and animal rights issues as well as regional separatist movements and global religious sects. Terrorists, like other criminals, can be individuals, small local gangs or large international organisations. Their level of sophistication, indeed the length of their very existence in one particular shape or form, can vary widely from long-established networks to temporary alliances over a single issue.

FATF Example 10: Raising of funds through a Not-For-Profit Organisation (NPO)

A registered charity, ostensibly involved in child welfare, used video tapes depicting religious "freedom fighters" in action in various countries, together with graphic images of atrocities perpetrated against members of that religion. The tapes contained an appeal to send donations to a post office box number to help in the "struggle". These tapes were apparently widely distributed around religious establishments throughout the region. The same post office box number was associated with a further appeal in magazines, which published articles by well known extremists.

The cost of mounting individual terrorist attacks may be very small, to the extent that an active cell member might be financed simply by means of a credit card. However, much larger sums must be assembled to fund recruitment and training, to buy equipment and information, support families, and to ensure a blind eye is turned to certain goings on.

International terrorist operations in this sense are only possible where a "finance department" can move substantial payments around a country or around the world. Funding may come in a few large amounts handled by a small number of trusted bankers. It may involve many small amounts handled by a wider range of people, wittingly or unwittingly.

FATF Example 11: NPOs used to make illegal transfers

An on-going criminal investigation into a network of foundations (at least 215 NPOs) established by the members of a particular immigrant community revealed that the network was transferring large sums of money regularly to a few accounts in another country. Suspicious transaction reports from the banks were triggered by the unusually high amount of the transactions in comparison with the stated purpose and activities of the foundations. After an initial analysis, it became clear that one of the beneficiaries of the transactions carried out by these organisations was a company contained in the UN Security Council list of designated persons. The FIU forwarded the case for further investigation by law enforcement agencies.

Although the stated purpose of these foundations was charitable, the size and frequency of the transfers (both through regular bank accounts and by using money transfer services) were difficult to explain. Over a 3-year period, the 35 NPOs sent over USD 160 million overseas. The network consisted of a sizable number of foundations spread throughout the country, with a concentration in cities with a large presence of the same immigrant community. The ongoing criminal investigation concluded that the NPOs were most likely a cover for an alternative remittance system.

Individuals, businesses and organisations sympathetic to the underlying cause may allow funds to pass through their account or simply make money available on request. Sometimes funds are processed by employees, who work without their bosses' knowing or not knowing until it is too late.

Knowledge of who undertakes terrorist financing is detailed in some areas but incomplete in others. Sometimes it is the same people who launder money relating to drugs and money related to terrorism—they probably don't even care or want to know what happens to the laundered funds, provided the price is right. It is not always possible to spot the different motives and methods of launderers, or to establish definite patterns.

Whole Organisations

In some cases, the focus on who is laundering money can be too detailed. Some of the most successful laundering has taken the form not of passing a single payment, but of a person "on the inside" passing a series of payments. Sometimes an entire organisation is set up as, or becomes, a wholesale money-laundering vehicle, embroiled (as in the case of BCCI) in widespread fraud and financial manipulation.

Much depends on the ability of businesses through which laundering takes place to spot unusual activity and the actors involved. Again, whether they like it or not, businesses are in the front line in protecting society.

FATF Example 12: Gold processing company used as a cover for money laundering

The money laundering organisation used a company processing and working gold to introduce cash from the sale of cannabis in Country R into the banking system of Country P. Moreover, the money launderers used a system that had been designed to make payments relating to cigarette smuggling and defraud Country P by applying for value added tax (VAT) refunds for non-existent operations.

The organisation had a person operating in Country R who collected bags full of sterling and other European currencies at restaurants and hotels near airports. The money came from the sale of cannabis in various European countries. The money was transported by air to Country P and declared in customs as payment for gold the company in Country P had sold to a company in Country R.

The various currencies were paid into bank accounts in a city in Country P, certifying the origin of the money by means of the customs declaration completed at the border. These sales of gold by the company in Country P to the company in Country R were fictitious, and they were documented by false invoices. Subsequently the gold was supposedly sold to a company in a nearby offshore location, which issued a false letter of receipt.

The fictitious gold sales made it possible to transport money in cash from Country R to Country P where it was deposited in banks. Furthermore, it enabled the money launderers to apply for a refund on the VAT supposedly paid.

In order for this mechanism to work the money launderers operated a gold working company which bought gold ingots from the largest metal wholesaler in Country P. Part of the gold was used to manufacture gold wire and shipped to Country F, where it was delivered to a finishing company that melted it back down and sold it, paying by bank transfer to the same banks in Country P. Another portion of the gold sold by the company was diverted onto the black market where it was sold without VAT and therefore at an advantageous price for its buyers.

To complete the circuit, given that the initial gold purchase from the wholesaler had not been subject to VAT, the organisation set up a group of companies run by front men who issued false invoices for the sale of gold on which VAT was applied.

The system used also enabled the organisation to change funds into the local currency and introduce them into the banking system. This money was used to pay transport costs and bribes relating to cigarette smuggling. The vehicles travelled through Country P but never reached their cities of destination in the neighbouring region.

Why is Money laundered?

Whilst as we have seen a Loan Shark can arrange cash to fund crimes and the Fence will dispose of the proceeds, they are expensive. If the Loan Shark charges 30% and the Fence charges 40%, then the remaining rewards to the criminal may not adequately compensate the risks involved in the underlying crime.

Fences and Loan Sharks might also attract attention, especially if they suddenly operate on a large scale, which would defeat the very purpose of using them. They may also simply betray the criminal to the police for a reward.

Only a specialist laundering operation offers a comparatively cheap and secure way of "washing" high value assets safely. The more sensitive the purpose of money laundering, the more important it is to have effective money laundering arrangements.

Getting "Precedes" together

Assembling the resources required to commit serious crimes can be complex and must clearly be discreet. Assets must be channelled from where they have been obtained or stored to where they are needed. Knowing what such resources comprise can help unsuspecting suppliers and service providers spot suspicious activity. Typical pre-crime expenses are:

- Premises in which to live and from which to operate
- Living expenses such as food, clothing, phone and internet connections, electricity
- Vehicles and other means of transport, such as flight tickets
- Photographic equipment
- Commercial identity card making equipment
- Laboratory equipment
- Company formation and secretarial services
- Vehicles adapted for carrying special (illicit) cargoes
- Ingredients of home-made explosives

They also include requirements that can only be met from underworld sources such as:

- False identity cards, passports and driving licences
- Arms, explosives and the "muscle" and "brains" to use them.

Money laundering transactions allow this shopping list to be filled without giving rise to suspicions about future crime or potential criminals.

Getting rid of the Evidence and getting out

Once a crime has given rise to proceeds, the criminal's main concern is to move money away from places where it might prove "too hot to handle" to places where it may be safely stored. Above all, the money is being laundered to erase any trail leading back to the crime or to the criminals.

This is done in the most convenient form possible, taking into account the cost and the risks of the method involved. Once the proceeds are safely channelled away they can be applied to further crime or safely used for the non-criminal purposes of everyday living.

Whether for getting resources together to commit a crime, or dispersing resources after a crime, it's all about criminals enabling themselves to do what they want, where and when they want—and covering the tracks.

Money launderers and the other criminals behind them don't care if money is laundered this way or that way, or who gets hurt in the process, so long as it works effectively, reasonably efficiently and doesn't lead back to them. This makes them potentially dangerous people when crossed or threatened.

Understanding the Big Picture—Six Key Points

It is precisely because different people see different facets of the money laundering cycle that there are many variations in people's understanding of the problem. But as has been seen, money laundering is basically " what criminals do to conceal assets linked to past or future crime". It is worthwhile keeping a number of the points covered so far in mind.

Point 1—More common than you think
Criminals either need resources to commit crime, or they commit crime because they need resources. Money laundering is thus as common as crime itself.

Point 2—Any Form
The asset can literally be *any resource or means of storing or transferring value*. An expensive watch, a car, a house, office equipment, a sports complex, a painting or the alleged receipts from a predominantly cash business such as dry-cleaning can all be a criminal asset. Whole companies can prove to be criminal assets, bought at arm's length by criminals with the proceeds of crime.

Point 3—Legal-looking business
Genuine business is the best cover for illegal assets. Money launderers dupe people who do not carry out basic checks and who fail to check further when suspicion is aroused. When the professional money launderer is at work, it's not appearances that you judge, it's reality.

Point 4—Seemingly Respectable People
The days of anonymous bank accounts, unlicensed casinos and non-existent pizza parlours as laundering loopholes are numbered in most reputable business centres. Money launderers now hide in the crowd, posing as reputable people doing reputable business to fool people into doing their dirty work for them.

Point 5—Clever Businesses Steer Clear
By the nature of the underlying crimes and the criminals involved, being vulnerable to involvement in money laundering puts money and reputation at risk. Because it is hard and expensive work to re-establish a good reputation and restore financial reserves, big businesses are prepared to invest significant amounts in anti-money laundering systems.

Point 6—Hard to Get Out.

People and businesses who get involved do not only risk goodwill and profitability. They may be putting themselves, their business and their family at physical risk as well. And if they don't attract unwanted attention from money launderers they will attract it from the authorities—probably both. So however you define money laundering, it means big trouble for those who knowingly or carelessly get mixed up in it.

The next chapter explores the last two points in more detail.

THREE

How does Money Laundering affect my Business?

Threats from Money Laundering

It's easy to think that money laundering only happens to other people. But because laundering can involve assets other than money and financial instruments, it is something *all* businesses need to be concerned about. *Any* unfortunate or unwary business can offer launderers cover for their operations.

For the businesses involved, the problem is not just that money laundering enables criminals and terrorists to operate. Rather, like a bad illness, it weakens the very structures it lives off. It can even destroy them – businesses, sectors and countries alike.

Ruining Businesses

When a business is thought or found to be involved in money laundering, risks start to mount quickly. As the business loses its reputation, customers shy away. Cash flow and credit lines disappear, raising the risk of insolvency. Meanwhile the business, its owners, directors and staff may become liable to civil claims and criminal charges. The criminals behind the money-laundering scheme may threaten violence and extort money.

It is important to remember that these are just the immediate results of being linked (rightly or wrongly) to money-laundering. There may also be other crimes involved, especially fraud, to make the money-laundering scheme work or to extract more profit. These risks, not least to staff whose jobs will be lost if the firm collapses, are discussed in more detail in the next Chapter.

Ruining Markets And Sectors

There are some simple economic arguments that show how money laundering upsets markets and the economies they serve. By the way money launderers operate, money laundering often creates false supply and demand for goods and services. The firms that launderers

"Dunno who you mean by Bona Fide, mate—who does he play for?"

establish trade primarily not for profit, but to create a cover for moving and storing criminal assets. So long as they are successful the criminal nature of their assets means that profit is assured. They can therefore afford to buy and sell goods at off-market rates and, in doing so, endanger legitimate businesses.

For example, a launderer buys carpets in Country A with illicit cash, and is therefore prepared to pay prices above normal market levels. By doing so he drives up the cost of carpets for honest buyers in Country A. He then transports the carpets legally to Country B where they are sold cheaply, so driving down the income of honest carpet sellers in Country B.

Sooner or later money launderers move on, either to avoid detection or to save money by using cheaper laundering alternatives. Those who sold him carpets in Country A suddenly find their market has dried up and those who bought in Country B are likewise left short of cheap supply. They can no longer trade, or can trade only at greatly increased cost or reduced income.

At the very least the market has been distorted. In the worst case honest buyers and sellers may be forced out of the market and consumer choice reduced.

Ruining Regions and Countries

The damage done at market level is reflected at higher levels, too. If one or more sectors of a market are tainted by money laundering (and it doesn't have to be many), the whole industry and even the country may soon get a reputation for bad business. Fearing volatile prices and shady dealing, important customers and trading partners lose confidence. They look for better regulated sectors and countries in which to do business.

Lost business is hard to replace as new clients and partners are understandably reluctant to establish or invest in a sector or country where money laundering is (or is rumoured to be) a risk. There doesn't have to be lots of money laundering going on for this to happen, just more than in competing sectors and regions.

Most worryingly, the prevalence of money laundering is taken as a sign of underlying crime. Regions and countries with high crime records are considered unpleasant to live in and often associated with poorly performing economies. These factors deter inward investors and make it hard to stimulate the economy. As growth stagnates there is increasing temptation for businesses to cut legal corners and a vicious circle becomes fully established. The downwards spiral in standards only makes things easier for criminals.

Scenarios for specific Businesses and Sectors

At any given time, one type of business may be more attractive than others to money launderers. Threats change with time and can be displaced from one area into another by a tough response. Indeed, as a result of greater awareness and stronger anti-money laundering regulation, financial institutions are on their guard against changes in money laundering patterns as never before.

Anti-money laundering measures are now being extended from financial institutions to other businesses and professions where high value transactions occur. These offer good cover for bad business and the chance to launder in size. They are targeted by criminals either as a direct way of laundering money or as a respectable gateway to the financial payments system.

Appendix 1 shows the types of businesses which, because they are thought to be at special risk, are usually covered by special money laundering regulations in addition to the general laws against money laundering which affect everyone.

Sometimes money launderers use the business or person they are targeting in a one-off money laundering exercise, such as buying and selling a work of art or an expensive car. At other times the intent may be to set up a longer lasting money laundering operation, for example by getting a lawyer to establish and run a company for them. The following scenarios show how specific businesses can be at risk:

Scenario 1: A small jewellery shop is exploited in a one-off transaction.

A jewellery shop in a regional town is approached by a client who explains that a relative has died, leaving some money and some jewels. The client has inherited the money and a poor cousin – with whom he has a bitter family feud – has inherited the jewels.

The client asks the jeweller to buy the jewels from the cousin and then sell them on to him. He offers a generous fee, fitting the delicacy of the situation and the sentimental value involved. The jeweller is given cash for the jewels and is asked for a bank transfer by the cousin.

Later, the police explain to the jeweller that the "client" and his "cousin" are, of course, part of the same gang that stole both cash and jewels.

Scenario 2: A large antique dealer becomes hooked.

The same gang moves on to a large town. "By chance" they meet the director of a large antique store. They tell a story very similar to the one above and the director is asked to undertake a very similar transaction to the one above.

However, when it is finished, the gang tells him that he has just helped them to launder money and show him shattering evidence. They tell him he must continue to help them by giving false receipts and invoices and trading antiques for cash and cheques, as they require. Otherwise they will denounce him anonymously to the police.

The director is forced to handle regular amounts of cash and issue false documentation, including foreign payment instructions. After eighteen months, the launderers disappear and the director is left trying to explain everything to the tax authorities.

Scenario 3: A real estate broker is exploited.

A middle-aged businessman approaches a small industrial real estate agency, run by an elderly gentleman. The businessman says he manages a number of rental properties in a neighbouring region. Can the agent take over some of the paper work – for a good fee, of course? A deal is reached.

The businessman collects the rent in cash weekly, and gives it to the estate agency for banking. The agency passes on a fixed amount to the property owners every month. The businessman also offers interior decoration services, which bring in a lot of money, again mostly in cash, but which do not make much profit. Most of the cash is used to pay invoices to subcontractors and suppliers – again, by giro transfer through the estate agent's account.

After a year or so, the businessman says he is moving on. Later the estate agent finds out that, strangely, the tenants, the property owners, the redecoration service and the suppliers have all moved on, too.

Scenario 4: A lawyer is bounced.

A firm of lawyers is approached by an import/export client for whom they have undertaken minor work in the recent past. The client would like to undertake an investment on behalf of foreign partners. The money is paid into the lawyers' client account a week in advance of the transaction in a single amount from a reputable bank.

The deal goes off smoothly and is repeated every few weeks. The amounts involved rise as the client claims "other foreign investors want a slice of the action". The money always comes from a reputable bank.

Some months later, the client asks the lawyer to prepare the largest deal so far. The money duly arrives but from a number of less well-known banks "to save time", the client claims. All the paper work is in place. Shortly before completion, the intended counterparty suddenly withdraws from the deal on a minor technicality.

The "investors" are soon demanding their money back and threatening to sue the client and the lawyers. The client asks the lawyer to refund the monies in the client account immediately, but not to the bank accounts from whence they came. The deals are never repeated, and shortly afterwards the import/export firm goes out of business.

Scenario 5: An accountant suffers short-sightedness.

An accountant is asked to keep the books for the new local branch of an overseas company, to open the necessary bank accounts and to act as temporary finance director. The local agent of the overseas company says they are keen to get going and that the money for the branch will arrive over the next few days.

It does, and not from one source but from many. The local agent says that too much has been paid in and that the overseas company wants the money transferred to where it was really wanted. Shortly after the agent says the branch opening will have to be delayed pending government licences being granted.

After several similar false starts, when the company eventually begins trading, the cash-flow seems to consist entirely of international payments to or from third parties without any sign of local business.

Meanwhile a bank has filed suspicious transaction reports. With the local agent suddenly gone, the accountant has a lot to explain.

Scenario 6: A tax adviser is badly advised

A tax adviser is asked to advise a small engineering consultancy on tax related matters. The consultancy, which does a lot of high value work in developing countries, receives a lot of money from associated companies in well-known tax havens.

The money is used to pay consultants and the tax advisers are asked to ensure the whole operation is tax efficient from the local angle, even down to claiming tax incentives for export-oriented firms. The tax adviser becomes suspicious when, despite a major earthquake in one of the company's major areas of operations, all work seems to be going on undisturbed.

However, the police in another country have already picked up on the company's activities elsewhere and advise their local counterparts. The adviser must avoid a charge of assisting in a tax fraud and facilitating money laundering.

The Moral of the Scenarios

These stories illustrate how easily an individual business can become the unwilling victim of direct money laundering operations. In each case, businesses trading with businesses used by launderers would also be liable to embarrasing and time-consuming investigation by the authorities. Unless you pick your clients and business partners well, you may become a direct or indirect victim of laundering.

FOUR

How am I vulnerable?

What makes me vulnerable to Money Laundering?

Money laundering schemes, like any other businesses, operate where conditions are most favourable. If a country or sector has tight money laundering controls, money laundering operations will shift to a less regulated sector or country, which still offers the necessary infrastructure.

Similarly, as a result of economic, fiscal or legal developments (whether or not associated with money laundering), a sector or individual business can suddenly find itself the unwanted target of money laundering groups.

Whilst background factors such as these are important, what goes on inside a business is critical and there are six important causes of vulnerability from within.

Ignorance and Indifference

If employees at any level of any business are ignorant about or ignore the risks of bad money, the business becomes an easy target. Thus the greatest vulnerability from money laundering is not related to a particular feature of an economic sector. It is related to a lack of understanding and action resulting either from ignorance, indifference or complacency.

Employees who are motivated to watch out for money laundering protect themselves, each other and the business. The more people in a business who know what money laundering is, how it arises, what form it can take and how to protect against it, the less chance that business has of running into trouble.

Lack of public and private sector Co-operation
The next vulnerability comes from businessmen thinking that stopping money laundering doesn't concern business and that it is a police matter in which they do not need to be involved.

Preventing vulnerability…

Unfortunately, it is hard for governments to tackle money laundering without reports of suspicious activity from businesses. Most public sector anti-money laundering effort is based on such reports combined with other intelligence leads. This avoids having to increase massively the number of inspection visits, which would only impede business even more.

The basic fact is that businesses are usually in a far better position to know what is normal in the day-to-day behaviour of customers than money laundering investigators. In turn investigators have wide powers (which businesses do not have) to look at what may be going on behind a suspicious activity, but they don't always know where to look. Only by working in co-operation can the one help the other to best effect.

Not documenting our business Activity

In any one country business is transacted both formally and informally. Formal business activity typically relies on documents such as references, contracts, invoices, receipts, cheques and statements of account. These provide a record of what happened, when it happened and which parties were involved.

Informal business is the simple exchange of goods and services for cash, or goods and services in kind. There is no formal documentation and thus no legally valid record of what has been transacted, though individuals may keep some form of private note as to what they have given or received. Trust is often an important element of such systems, for example where the assets involved are exchanged elsewhere or a third party is involved in another way.

Informal systems still exist in street markets in developed countries and they are often the dominant system in emerging economies where literacy and numeracy are low and formal systems are seen as barriers to trade. However, countries where large sums flow between informal and formal systems attract the attention of international criminals and, sooner or later, international authorities.

Forgetting simple Checks

A fourth vulnerability comes from failing to do the simple checks that can help detect money laundering. The senior management of a firm must check that people in the business are doing what they are supposed to do to stop money laundering. This means checking that clients and transactions and staff, including the senior managers, are acting in good faith.

Lack of Systems

A fifth vulnerability comes from accepting the need for awareness and co-operation yet *not putting into place the policies, procedures and practices needed.* It may often be just a matter of applied common sense, but it still has to be done.

Ignoring possible Threats

The sixth and last vulnerability comes from thinking it is not possible to plan for the unexpected. In business, the unexpected can and does occur. Whilst a precise event cannot be predicted, knowing where to go for information, advice and help to reduce its potential impact can usually be established well in advance and relatively easily (see Appendix 2 Sources of Help).

How do Vulnerabilities hit Home?

Chapter 3 highlighted damage done by money laundering to whole business sectors and countries. When vulnerabilities of an individual business are exposed, the consequences of laundering hit close to home.

For an individual business, involvement in money laundering can lead to:

- *Loss of reputation* If the reputation of the business is tarnished by even unwitting association with wrong doing, it may take years to get a good reputation back again, if indeed at all. This is especially the case if the business is based on trust. Only a few of the partners in Arthur Andersen, the accountancy firm, were caught up in the Enron scandal, yet the world-wide organisation collapsed as a result of the loss of trust. The firm's client base vanished.
- *Loss of credit and credit standing.* As clients disappear so does cash-flow, which means that creditors become nervous. Banks may call

in loans for fear of bad debts. Credit rating agencies will downgrade the company meaning it will be charged higher interest rates on its borrowings. Credit scoring agencies may also place warnings against the business making it harder to obtain goods and services on credit.

- *Lower valuation or share price.* A business tainted by scandal will lose goodwill and be seen as a higher risk. The failure to manage money laundering risk may call into question management's judgement in other areas, all of which may be reflected in a lower share price (if it is a listed company) or a lower sale price (if it is a privately held one).

- *Staff defection* Key staff may decide the only way to preserve their personal reputations is to find another employer. They may well take key customers with them.

Seen in these terms it is easy to see how the uncontrollable downward spiral leading to an Enron or Andersen-type collapse comes about. The effects can be devastating for individuals as well:

Laid off…

- *Loss of earnings and redundancy.* Loss of earnings results from lower sales, profit and reserves. Staff may have to be laid off
- *Dismissal.* The only way to restore confidence in the management of a business hit by money laundering may be to replace key members of staff
- *Blackmail and threats of violence.* Even if you want to get out of a relationship with money launderers, they may not want to let you do so. Threats against a person or their family members may or may not be followed through
- *Professional misconduct charges.* Professional organisations take an increasingly intolerant view of behaviour that brings the sector into disrepute. Individuals may face disciplinary proceedings with sanctions that include the loss of professional recognition and thus their whole career.

Both businesses and individuals thought or found to be connected with money laundering are highly likely to have regulatory, legal and fiscal problems that are both difficult and expensive to resolve.

- *Close attention from enforcement agencies.* Be they a sector regulator or the police, those with responsibility for enforcing anti-money laundering rules take their duties very seriously. Firms and their employees under suspicion will face detailed questioning about their actions and, even if no evidence of involvement is found, they may remain subject to tight surveillance until such time as the enforcement agency is satisfied there is no risk. This may take months or even years
- *Seizure of assets.* Courts may seize and freeze assets thought to be connected to money laundering. This includes financial and non-financial assets in the widest sense (or "instrumentalities" as they are called) used to launder money as well as assets being laundered. Where suspected criminal assets cannot be seized, courts may freeze legal assets of equivalent value, on their own initiative or at the request of a foreign jurisdiction. If money laundering is proven the assets can be confiscated

- *Civil penalties.* An institution subject to regulation may be said by the regulator to have violated anti-money laundering rules. If it wishes, without admitting or denying guilt, to avoid a potentially damaging court case, the institution may have to pay a sizeable civil penalty. Since January 2004 three financial institutions have agreed civil penalties of $10 million, $25 million and $24 million with the US regulator FinCEN in respect of shortcomings identified by FinCEN in their AML arrangements

- *Criminal procedures.* Key employees will face questioning and possible arrest. Charges of failure to report suspicions, or indeed of money laundering itself, may be brought with a trial, adverse publicity and possibly a fine and/or prison term to follow

- *Civil litigation.* Company executives may be sued by the victims of the offence underlying the money laundering.[1] They may also face action from investors for failure to exercise due care and from staff for failing to shield them from threats and blackmail

- *Extradition.* If the offence is serious enough individuals may find themselves subject to extradition and trial in another country. It may only be necessary for a payment to pass through a foreign country or a foreign financial institution for those involved with the payment to come under the relevant foreign country's jurisdiction.[2] The extent of involvement may simply be that they are an official of a company involved in the payment. Allegations of involvement corruption and terrorist offences, however tangential, can add a whole new dimension to the issue.

- *Additional tax demands.* There may be a lengthy tax inspection of the business and key individuals. Tax demands can arise where unexplained income is found or expenses are reviewed and disallowed.

- *Costly legal fees.* Representation in litigation, criminal cases and professional tribunals as well as tax advice will typically involve high fees.

Any one of these risks is reason enough for employees at all levels to want to protect themselves and their colleagues from the risk of money laundering. Taken together they put paid to the notion that involvement in money laundering is a minor matter which can always be sorted out. Even if a business or person is able eventually to find a way out of all of the above, they will have paid a heavy personal cost in time, money and emotional energy.

The ultimate Aim—reducing underlying Crime

At the root of the fight against money laundering is the attempt to avoid the crime and the lawlessness that gives rise to money laundering. Such crimes often have effects greater than the immediate negative impacts of money laundering itself.

Whilst there is much debate about the link between stopping money laundering and stopping crime, most countries' crime reduction policy is based on the view that the easier it is to launder money, the greater the risk of crime.

People and businesses that do not tackle money laundering risks increase their overall exposure, and that of their community, to becoming direct victims of crimes against the person and against property.

The greatest reward from preventing money laundering is helping to create a just and safe society in which honest people and honest businesses can thrive. The value of such an environment is priceless.

NOTES:

1. In some jurisdictions, victims of money laundering may have a statutory right to bring civil proceedings.
2. This is particularly the case with the long-arm jurisdiction of US courts (see Chapter 5).

FIVE

Responses to Money Laundering

Economic Rationale for Legislation

Whilst many people accept the need to prevent money laundering as a matter of common sense it is also useful to understand how international conventions and laws have been introduced to control money laundering.

Apart from the need to fulfil treaty obligations, the strongest objective arguments for co-ordinated international action are that:

- The effects of money laundering, like the crimes behind it, are too damaging to leave protection to chance.
- Common legal minimum standards ensure equal standards apply nationally and internationally
- Conventions can establish common levels of regulation across the world and so deny money launderers safe havens for their operations.

Conventions and laws do not simply create costs. They also create benefits for honest businesses, their customers, owners and staff. International conventions have placed an obligation on governments to enforce anti-money laundering laws. If governments fulfil these obligations they protect good businesses against unfair competition from bad ones. They also ensure that bad businesses do not endanger the reputation of their sector (or indeed themselves) by lax or inadequate anti-money laundering procedures.

Some of the requirements of anti-money laundering laws may in any case simply be good practice. For example, knowing who one's client really is helps to establish if they may be a source of further deals or a lead to other customers.

Many states look closely at the cost benefit of anti-money laundering regulations to make sure there are net benefits of regulation. Secondary benefits include a reduction in fraud and an increase in the understanding of a client's business that can lead to more profitable sales. On a national scale these side effects can generate substantial gains both for the whole economy and individual firms.

International legal and industry Standards

UN, IMF and FATF

In a world divided over many issues, there has been considerable unity in efforts to detect money laundering as a way to disrupt and deter the underlying crime. As previously described, the key concerns are drug trafficking, organised crime, fraud and terrorism. Much of the impetus for anti-money laundering regulation comes from global organisations, especially the United Nations (UN), International Monetary Fund/World Bank (IMF/IRBD) and Financial Action Task Force (FATF).

Since the 1980s, the UN has established a series of conventions and passed resolutions containing measures to combat money laundering and terrorist financing. These include the 1988 Vienna Convention, the 1999 Convention on the Suppressing of the Financing of Terrorism, General Resolution 51/210 and UN Security Council Resolution 1373.

The IMF has recently integrated assessment of anti-money laundering measures into its monitoring of the world's economies and developed a methodology to help determine how effectively countries are dealing with the problem. Its findings are included in the Reports on Standards and Codes that it publishes on individual countries on a periodic basis.

The methodology was developed with the help of FATF. This is a special intergovernmental body set up by the G7 Summit in 1989 to combat money laundering. Located in Paris, FATF itself now has over thirty member countries.

In 1990 FATF published its "40 Recommendations" on the prevention of money laundering, which were revised in 2003. After the 9/11 attacks in the USA it published the "Special 8" recommendations on combating terrorist financing. Together with a ninth Special Recommendation targeting cash smuggling in terrorist finance and terrorist funding (published in October 2004) the two sets of recommendations set the standard for global anti-money laundering and terror finance regulation and enforcement.

FATF also studies how money laundering occurs throughout the world and publishes annual Typologies Reports. The case studies used to illustrate these reports are also used as examples in this Guide.

There are a number of associated regional FATF-style task forces covering other parts of the world with their own membership and regional recommendations for the prevention of money laundering (see Appendix 2).

International peer review teams from the IMF, FATF and regional task forces mentioned above report regularly on how effectively individual countries are tackling money laundering. Their aim is to help responsible countries identify and correct weaknesses in anti-money laundering efforts. Their visits also allow countries where progress has been slow to learn what remedial action is indicated.

Countries that do not take firm action against money laundering can be subject to intense diplomatic pressure and, ultimately, economic sanctions such as the withholding of aid or additional controls on business transactions with that country.

Financial Institutions

It is often said that financial institutions are in the "front line" of the fight against money laundering (see Chapter 7). This is why global industry standards have been laid down by international organisations including the Basel Committee on Banking Supervision, the

International Association of Insurance Supervisors and the International Organisation of Securities Commissions.

Some sub-sectors of the financial industry have also developed their own more or less stringent voluntary standards, of which the Wolfsberg Group's Principles on private banking are probably the best known.

Professional Bodies

With the recognition that money laundering also occurs through service providers in the professions, the international co-ordinating bodies of the leading professions have also responded by establishing working parties, publishing guidelines and offering various forms of support to national professional associations.

This is important to note as in some countries national associations may have statutory duties under national money laundering legislation and the international association can help provide them with technical assistance.

The International Bar Association and the International Federation of Accountants are examples of two such global associations (details of which are given in Appendix 2) that develop and maintain anti-money laundering standards for their respective sectors.

As money launderers exploit the differences between the legal and industrial standards of differing business sectors and countries, co-ordination of standards at global industry level is important to prevent money launderers targeting a particular country or industry or operating in one country from the safety of another.

Common Features of national Laws

Core regulatory Issues

Different countries have different legal systems, so responsibilities for preventing money laundering may lie in different places according to national regulatory systems and style. However, as they follow international standards, anti-money laundering regulations in most countries ultimately focus on the same core issues. These are typically:

- What constitutes money laundering
- Underlying offences that give rise to money laundering
- Business activities subject to special anti-money laundering regulation
- Individuals subject to special anti-money laundering regulation
- Public and private sector bodies responsible for tackling money laundering
- When a business relationship or transaction commences
- When client identification must be undertaken or renewed
- Obligations to establish "beneficial owners", i.e. the real beneficiary of a business relationship or transaction, not just the "front man" or agent
- Acceptable proof of identity
- Business that is prohibited without client identification
- Reporting requirements regarding suspicious transactions
- Protection for those making reports
- Data protection issues
- Penalties for those breaking the law
- Internal procedures to support anti-money laundering efforts

Financial Intelligence Units

FATF standards require that countries have a central unit that receives and processes reports of suspicious activity as well as useful information from other sources. Such units are called Financial Intelligence Units or FIUs for short. They are responsible for collecting, analysing and disseminating information on money laundering for the purposes of investigation, prosecution and responding to requests from national and foreign authorities.

Some FIUs are part of the police or public prosecution service, whilst others are administrative. They may also have responsibilities for handling requests for information to and from other countries. An international network of around 100 national FIUs, called the Egmont Group, helps to maintain standards for the operation of FIUs and the exchange of data between them.

Common Provisions

Though the precise way in which legislation is framed varies from country to country, the normal function of such laws and regulations is to:

- Define money laundering as utilising assets relating to past or future criminal acts in order to conceal their origin, *or* engaging in certain types of transactions relating to such assets
- State that all crime of a certain gravity gives rise to money laundering, or list the relevant predicate offences in a schedule
- Define money laundering as a crime in itself
- Provide a schedule of the business activities subject to money laundering legislation and give definitions of these activities where doubt exists
- Entrust supervision and enforcement of key parts of the law to sector regulators and professional bodies
- Set limits and conditions for undertaking and recording transactions of a cash or non-cash nature
- Set out penalties for laundering negligently or with intent
- Require reporting suspicion of money laundering within a certain time limit and in a prescribed form
- Empower a special unit (the FIUs described above) to receive and process these reports
- State how business may be conducted after a report is made
- Set out penalties for failure to report suspicions

- Require a person to be appointed as the link between the business and the special unit (Money Laundering Reporting Officer)
- Require a person to be appointed to oversee compliance with anti-money laundering legislation (Compliance Officer)
- Set out arrangements to keep reports confidential
- Provide anonymity and legal protection to those reporting suspicions in good faith
- Set out record keeping requirements, including recovery of evidence in a legally admissible form
- Set out awareness and training requirements
- Specify the national standards for due diligence when identifying and accepting customers
- Set out rules for the identification and monitoring of higher risk accounts and managing special risks
- Specify how rules apply on a consolidated basis, e.g. with regard to the parent bank or head office and foreign branches and subsidiaries.

Sector Guidelines and in-house Rules

Sector Guidelines

Where sector regulators and professional bodies are responsible for supervising anti-money laundering arrangements they usually draw up their own specialised set of rules. The rules state the overall high level approach that is to be followed (e.g. a risk-based approach) and/or detailed action required. They may also produce a set of guidelines to assist firms in interpreting both the underlying legislation and such rules.

These guidelines set out specific procedures that businesses must follow in key areas such as account opening, cash handling, reporting, record-keeping and training. For example, where businesses must establish their own formal in-house systems and procedures to prevent money laundering, the guidelines may specify the nature of such arrangements, in terms of scope and, sometimes, level of detail.

Sector bodies normally offer training to raise awareness and to provide the specific skills needed to implement appropriate systems at the firm level. There may also be an anti-money laundering help desk or contact point that deals with questions about establishing anti - money laundering systems (as opposed to inquiries about possible suspicious transactions).

In-house Rules

Internal anti-money laundering procedures are another set of important norms. They lay out the precise operating procedures to be followed in a given firm to prevent money laundering. They cover, for example, what to do when examining client identity documents, who is to be informed when reporting a suspicion internally, when and what training is to be undertaken, as well as who is responsible for reports, records and their safekeeping.

Whilst this may seem a lot of rules and regulations, it is in fact the process by which very general laws for everyone are made into specific ptrocedures for specific cases. The important thing to bear in mind is which rules apply to your area, or areas like yours, and to focus on the basic messages, namely:

- Identify clients properly
- If you can't identify clients properly, don't deal with them
- Establish reliable internal controls and audit procedures
- Monitor accounts and transactions continually
- Keep records and keep them up-to-date
- If you have suspicions, report them
- Establish and maintain high standards of integrity
- Remember the importance of training
- Don't get involved with clients whose business you don't know
- Avoid cash transactions if your type of business allows.

In-house rules are discussed in more detail later.

Enforcement Issues

Criminal Penalties and Enforcement

National money laundering laws also set out the penalties for involvement in money laundering. These vary from country to country but three points are worthy of special mention here:

- There are often higher penalties for those in positions of trust and vulnerable sectors of the economy
- In some countries the penalties for money laundering are tougher than the penalty for the underlying crime
- When the money laundering involved is related to terrorism, then the penalties can be much more severe.

As time moves on, the attitudes of regulators to transgression is hardening, especially regarding financial institutions. In the mid- and late nineties it was understood that there was a learning curve for such businesses and a lead-time for installing the necessary systems. Many regulators are now basing enforcement policy on the fact that regulations have been around long enough for them to be understood and obeyed. They are imposing tough sanctions accordingly.

This tendency will only increase as countries try to demonstrate a convincing record of enforcement and thus the effectiveness of their anti-money laundering systems. The approach will be extended to other business sectors, with examples made of individual firms to encourage others to comply.

Internationalisation of criminal Enforcement

Globalisation of the world's economies has increased their vulnerability to foreign-based threats and threats against their foreign-based assets, both physical and intellectual.

There is increasing co-operation among nations to counter such threats, including mutual assistance with other countries' criminal investigations and extraditing those suspected of involvement in crime. Law enforcers and courts in one jurisdiction may use their own powers to assist an investigation or legal process originating in another. As a consequence, national criminal justice systems are extending their reach to persons and events outside their borders.

Universal Jurisdiction

As well as the increasing willingness of nations to afford mutual assistance national legislation now often criminalises terrorist financing wherever it occurs. This allows countries to take action against persons or organisations based in a second country in respect of suspected offences in a third country.

This is also the effect of some money laundering legislation, e.g. the US Foreign Corrupt Practices, Computer Fraud and Abuse, Economic Espionage, Bank Secrecy, Patriot and Sarbanes/Oxley Act all of which have reach outside the USA. The Financial Services and Modernization Act 2000 and the Patriot Act give US authorities powers that can be used to regulate the global activities of both US and non-US entities.

These acts and similarly structured legislation in other countries can be invoked even where the alleged mischief only has incidental links to the jurisdiction, such as the passage of a payment or e-mail through that jurisdiction. Concern has also been expressed that some legislation leads to both nationals and foreign nationals in a given country being liable to prosecution elsewhere for activities that were or are perfectly legal in the place where they occurred.

The main point however is that, where a business is unwittingly part of a money laundering scheme and that scheme in some way involves a jurisdiction with a proactive enforcement policy, the employees of that business may end up facing charges in, and extradition to, another country.

SIX

Using Regulations, Guidelines, Internal Systems and Procedures

Chapter 5 described how anti-money laundering legislation is normally written to cover a wide range of business activities, and how more specific anti-money laundering arrangements are made at industry sector and firm level.

Chapter 6 looks at some of the obligations common to anti-money laundering rules as they are implemented across all sectors and outlines the key principles of self-help. Chapter 7 looks at sector-specific issues.

If you have not done so already, you should establish now which legal, industry and professional guidelines apply to you and read them carefully. If in any doubt you should obtain proper advice (see Appendix 2 for sources of help).

Note that in this chapter the words "business" or "firm" mean a business or firm that is subject to money laundering regulations.

Drawing up internal Systems and Procedures

As seen in the previous chapter, anti-money laundering legislation world-wide usually requires those regulated to draw up internal anti-money laundering systems and procedures. Often, a prescribed format and sample text are published. Each business can then base its internal policies on the relevant text, with appropriate modifications to suit its own circumstances and internal working practices.

Where no set format is given, and a business must or wants to set up internal policies and procedures, one option is to track the format of the underlying primary or secondary legislation and guidelines. The internal practices should set out the action required in respect of each of the topics set out in the relevant legislation. Alternatively, the model rules for a similar sector can be adapted with changes made as the context requires and professional advice sought as needed.

Regulated businesses may have to submit internal policies and procedures to the relevant government or industry body for approval, and will almost certainly have to keep them available for inspection, if only as evidence of compliance with any duty to have anti-money laundering arrangements in place. When finished, internal policies and procedures should be widely distributed across the organisation.

Thereafter the policies and procedures will need to be reviewed on a regular basis for effectiveness and efficiency. They will probably need fine-tuning after a trial period. There may be a legal requirement to have them audited by a firm of experts.

Firms are well advised to consult with both the regulators and those who will use the policies and procedures whilst they are being drawn up. This will help improve both the quality of policies and procedures and the level of compliance. Again, drawing up policies and procedures requires careful thought and if you are not sure about what to do or how to go about it you should seek professional advice.

Drawing up and devising internal policing is a senior management responsibility. It should be clearly allocated to one of the firm's principal officers and closely monitored by other principals. Many firms nominate the finance or legal director to take responsibility for money laundering issues.

Training Staff

Reflecting typical national regulations and industry guidelines, in-house rules should specify mandatory training requirements in varying degrees of detail. When internal systems and procedures are being drawn up, it is important that a training strategy is established at the same time. Typically an in-house strategy should cover:

- The nature of training required
- How often it must be carried out
- How it is to be delivered
- Who must be trained
- Training records that must be kept
- Handling feed back
- Keeping training up to date and relevant

If a business does not know its obligations under law and if staff do not know where to look, what to look for or how to look at it, then spotting unusual transactions is largely a matter of luck, and money laundering is unlikely be prevented. Regular informed training is thus no mere formality, but the best chance of prevention there is.

Training covers two main areas. One is the specific procedures and tasks of everyone in the organisation, and how they are to be executed. The other concerns general awareness of the risks of money laundering and the ability to recognise unusual and suspicious activity. The first type of training is often linked closely to the work of a particular employee or group of employees, whilst the second may be more general and include awareness-raising campaigns as well as training on specific themes.

Good training is not a one-off event but a process that is carried on continually and reactively, being regularly updated to reflect both new threats and developments in prevention. Done properly, it should be motivational, helping those trained to value and use the skills they have obtained and take pride in their contribution to a safe work place.

It is useful (and in some jurisdictions a regulatory requirement) for firms to document anti-money laundering training procedures and content. It is essential that staff have access to adequate and timely training and to quality training material. If they are active in areas of high risk, additional specialist detailed training should be given.

Identifying Customers

Identification and Re-identification

Customer identification is the corner stone of anti-money laundering compliance. To comply with the law as it stands in most countries, regulated businesses can only enter a business relationship or conclude a transaction with people and organisations whose identity has been positively established at the outset.

The legal definition of a business relationship may differ between country and sector and may be different for money laundering purposes than for other purposes. This is where detailed reading of sector guidelines and their careful transposition into in-house systems and procedures (where necessary with professional guidance) is important.

Likewise national laws and sector guidelines typically set out what constitutes client identification in the compliance sense and the actions and documents that are acceptable for statutory identification purposes. Such details should also be incorporated into internal arrangements.

It is never too soon to think about the nature of a client contact, and whether it may (or already has led) to a business or customer relationship in the eyes of the law. Good knowledge of client identity is equally important as the relationship progresses – money launderers often exploit trust by carefully building up relationships over time. FATF recommends that client identification standards also be applied regularly to existing customers on the basis of materiality and risk.

What comes around finally goes around. For the purposes of record keeping it is therefore also important to know the legal definition of when a relationship has ended.

Timing of Identification and Reporting

Establishing client identity early on is important for all businesses, whether financial institutions or not. However, the law recognises that in some fast moving sectors this may not always be possible. Thus, although financial institutions are generally required to identify customers before opening an account or selling a financial product, in certain circumstances checks may take place as soon as possible thereafter. In most countries client identification requirements also include obtaining details as to the source of funds and the intended use of the account.

In most countries similar identification requirements already apply, or soon will apply, to businesses dealing in high value goods that handle cash. For example, an auctioneer, car dealer, yacht broker, real estate agent or jeweller will need to perform identification of the client if they:

- Enter into, or are in, a business relationship *or*
- Conclude a contract, *and*
- Accept cash payment above a certain value

The cash transaction values above which FATF recommends mandatory customer identification are:

- Financial Institutions (occasional customers) USD/EUR 15,000
- Casinos and Internet Gaming Houses USD/EUR 3,000
- Traders in precious metals and stones USD/EUR 15,000

Individual countries set different limits, which may differ according to the perceived risk of the transaction type (e.g. cash related wire transfer). Such limits must be applied to both single transactions and to smaller sized transactions that appear linked.

In many countries professionals are required to undertake identification of new clients at the time of entering into a business relationship, an event which in law may be before an initial contract or transaction is executed. Identification of existing customers who have not yet been formally identified must usually take place upon the next personal contact, or when entering into the next contract or transaction.

Client Due Diligence and Re-identification

One way to implement robust client identification is (where practical) to conclude separate contracts for each transaction or assignment, and check client identity each time. Another way is for firms to conduct periodic detailed background checks on clients as a matter of good business practice.

If at any time in the setting-up or conduct of a business relationship unusual or suspicious transactions arise there may be legal requirements for a report to be made to the authorities. If suspicions arise during the course of a business relationship, it may be necessary or advisable to repeat client identification, as part of a robust Customer Due Diligence process

Customer Due Diligence (CDD) is a term usually applied to describe the wider series of checks, which may consist of:

- Re-identifying and verifying customer identity with the help of reliable independent sources
- Double checking credentials and stories presented by agents on behalf of ultimate clients
- Establishing or confirming in detail the purpose and likely scope of a client's business
- Checking on the ongoing business transacted for consistency with expected business patterns and sources of funds.

Identify Or Decline

Identification of Individuals

The identification requirements for individuals (sometimes called *"natural"* persons) normally consist of at least two, and often several, original documents. In some jurisdictions the documents must be produced in person in a formal identification procedure.

Proper identification means that official documents presented must always be carefully checked. Detailed training and guidance notes may be necessary to ensure such checks are effective. If a client cannot be properly identified because he or she cannot provide the information required, or the information is contradictory, it is probably illegal to proceed with the relationship or transaction. If you have suspicions about money laundering you may have an obligation to make a report even though no business is transacted.

Having established the client's identity, it is important to check the client is not on any national government or industry black list of dubious individuals (e.g. banned directors). Checks should also be made on whether they are operating from one of the high risk countries listed from time to time by individual governments and international organisations such as FATF (as a Non Co-operative Country or Territory) and OECD (tax havens).

Checks also need to be made on the lists of known terrorists, terrorist organisations and other criminals published by various governments and international organisations around the world. Appendix 2 gives details of these lists and other sources of help in screening clients.

Identification at a Distance and Clients from Abroad

Where a client cannot or will not be identified in person (for example an on-line banking account or credit card client) there are normally alternative procedures such as postal identification. It may also be possible to rely on identification by approved third parties with whom the client has already successfully completed identification. However, it is important to establish not only if it is legal but also whether it is wise to rely on third party identification procedures in the given circumstances.

"And I thought we were relying on your identification...."

Identification required by law for foreign natural persons may differ from that required of domestic natural persons, but the underlying principles will be basically the same. Where the client does not appear personally to be identified, there are usually strict rules regarding the notarisation and authentication of identity documents and the identification of the client's local agent.

The procedures for both of the above situations are typically covered in detail in sector guidelines and should be reflected in internal guidelines.

Legal Persons

There are many possible forms of associations (or "corporate vehicles") through which business may be conducted. In addition to the traditional forms of sole trader, partnership and joint stock company, there are new structures which more effectively meet their members' needs and objectives, such as limited liability partnerships and economic interest groupings.

As well as vehicles which actually undertake business – buying, selling or providing services, there are vehicles established for legal or fiscal reasons, often known as "special purpose vehicles" or "special purpose entities" (SPV/SPE). These may be set up for any number of reasons – to hold assets or to obtain a perfectly legal form of tax status. Similar arrangements are sometimes made to qualify for grants and subsidies, again perfectly legally.

However, most complex money laundering involves the abuse of corporate vehicles, and schemes involving SPVs are often used to undertake money laundering, fraud and tax evasion. It pays to be especially careful in establishing the identity of the natural business partners when dealing with legal persons.

ID for legal Persons such as Firms, Clubs and Charities.

Where the customer is a public or private sector body such as a company, a partnership or a not-for-profit association (or "*legal person*") it is necessary to establish the identity and authority of:

- The natural person(s) signing the contract
- Anyone named as a contact in any contract

The client should be asked to produce reliable types of recent official registration documentation not older than, say, 30 days. These should give details of legal status, the name and addresses of key officers and owners of the legal person (e.g. shareholders, trustees, directors) and any articles regarding how the association can be bound by the actions of its employees and officers. Photocopies or other acceptable form of record should be kept.

It is not usually necessary to identify the owners of a public company that is subject to regulatory disclosure requirements and quoted on a recognised exchange.

Overseas legal Persons

The same type of information and identification for overseas legal persons should be obtained as for domestic ones. Registration documentation and document presentation requirements will be different because international registration practices differ. Again, it is necessary to identify the local agents of foreign legal persons according to the procedures for identifying local clients.

Simplified Procedures

Checking every transaction all of the time may be impossible or at least highly inefficient given that anti-money laundering measures are meant to target high-risk transactions. Where local regulations allow, and the risk profile of a customer and transaction is low, it may be possible to rely on the anti-money laundering measures established by law and custom in each country when undertaking due diligence.

Examples of customers presenting low risks where simplified procedures may be permissible include:

- Financial institutions subject to money laundering regulation and supervision
- Public sector departments and enterprises

Chapter 7 discusses some specific grounds for simplified due diligence. However, always remember that where simplified due diligence leads to suspicion, then the grounds for maintaining simplified due diligence have clearly disappeared!

Monitoring

Generally speaking, once due diligence has been performed, the results may be relied on until doubts arise or a specific period of time has passed. This may be as a result of new information coming to light, e.g. as a result of routine credit checks, press articles, market intelligence or a change in the pattern of business, which is inconsistent with expectations. Such expectations will depend largely on the customer's business profile.

Special Considerations

Politically Exposed Persons

Politically Exposed Persons or "PEP"s are essentially people prominent in the public life of a country and in its institutions. They include senior judges, politicians, political party members, high-ranking civil servants, military officials or heads of state owned industry.

Those who are PEPs by virtue of their respective positions in one particular country remain PEPs in any country where they are economically active. A relative or close associate of a PEP can also be a PEP by acting on the PEP's behalf.

Senior Managers should sign off on acceptance…

The links between PEPs and possible money laundering are usually corruption, theft of public property and tax avoidance, all of which are typically crimes against the state. But PEPs also commit crimes against people and businesses in the form of fraud and embezzlement. Whilst some countries have almost endemic corruption, FATF is quick to point out that few countries have no corruption at all.

FATF Example 13: A senior government official launders embezzled public funds via members of his family.

The family of a former Country A senior government official, who had held various political and administrative positions, set up a foundation in Country B, a fiscally attractive financial centre, with his son as the primary beneficiary. This foundation had an account in Country C from which a transfer of approximately USD 1.5 million was made to the spouse's joint account opened two months previously in a banking establishment in neighbouring Country D. This movement formed legitimate grounds for this banking establishment to report a suspicion to the national FIU.

The investigations conducted on the basis of the suspicious transaction report found a mention on this same account of two previous international transfers of substantial sums from the official's wife's bank accounts held in their country of origin (A). The wife held accounts in other national banking establishments also provisioned by international transfers followed by withdrawals.

The absence of any apparent economic justification for the banking transactions conducted and information obtained on the initiation of legal proceedings against the senior government official in his country for embezzlement of public funds led to the presumption, in this particular case, of a system being set up to launder the proceeds of this crime. The official concerned was subsequently stopped for questioning and placed in police custody just as he was preparing to close his bank account.

Businesses undertaking client identification will need to establish a system to decide if a client is politically exposed, and obtain senior management approval before accepting them fully as clients. The source of wealth and source of funds for PEPs, their relatives and associates must be checked and the relationship subject to special monitoring.

Though illegal activities by PEPs may be suspected, they can be hard to prove. A PEP may enjoy legal immunity or be able to influence prosecutorial and judicial decision-making. Their activities may also be fronted by associates or hidden behind a corporate veil of offshore companies. The extent of their activities may only come to light on a change of government, through leaks by political opponents or when an associate is careless. The illegal activities of General Sani Abacha are a good example of this.

PEPs can also use their position to fund political, including terrorist, interests. This may include trying to take advantage of diplomatic immunity. However, most reputable countries do not use diplomatic immunity as an excuse to avoid "ordinary" anti-money laundering regulation, let alone measures to combat terrorism. An attempt to use diplomatic immunity in such cases is a danger signal in itself.

Backhanders

FATF Example 14: A senior employee of a state-owned company involved in high level corruption

An investigation into a senior government official Mr. A, an employee of state owned Company A, uncovered that he was in receipt of excessive payments into a number of accounts that he owned and operated. Mr. A was the vice president of Company A and had a yearly income of over USD 200,000. The investigation revealed Mr. A had 15 bank accounts in several different countries through which over USD 200 million had been transacted. Mr. A used the money placed in these accounts to gain political influence and to win large contracts from foreign governments on behalf of Company A.

The investigation discovered that a trust account had been created to act as conduit through which payments from Company A were then transferred to a number of smaller accounts controlled by Mr. A. Mr. A would then transfer money from these accounts or make cash withdrawals. The funds, once withdrawn were used to pay for bribes. The recipients of these payments included: heads of state and government, senior government officials, senior executives of state owned corporations and important political party officials in several countries and family members and close associates of Mr. A.

Further investigation into the financial transactions associated with the accounts held by Mr. A revealed that a shell company was being used to make and receive payments. In addition to this regular account activity, there were irregular cash deposits (often more than one a day) and unusually large of cash withdrawals; one account revealed that in one six week period over USD 35 million had been withdrawn in cash. This was inconsistent with all the previous activity on the account. The investigators noticed that there was also a deliberate smurfing of the cash deposits into smaller amounts indicating Mr. A had an awareness of reporting requirements and was attempting to avoid them. The beneficial owners of payments from Mr. A made both in cash and by wire transfer implicated several PEPs and associates of PEPs.

Offshore financial Centres

The 1980's and 1990's saw a large growth in the number and activities of what are known as "offshore financial centres" (OFCs) Many OFCs are small islands, and those with well established and well regulated financial services industries are widely recognised as genuine players in global business markets. The move towards the provision of reputable financial services has helped support what are often weak or non-existent economies. The IMF estimates that just over 40 OFCs hold the equivalent of around 50 percent of total cross-border assets.

However, some OFCs have lacked the resources and political will to regulate conduct of business in line with international standards. In particular they have been heavily criticised for offering tax regimes which distort trade and investment patterns and lower the tax income of "onshore" countries. Estimates of assets held beyond the reach of effective taxation are as high as around one-third of total global gross domestic product, the value of goods and services. Some of this is constituted by proceeds of offences related to tax evasion.

The key issue however is that some OFCs have also been directly criticised for facilitating money laundering. Studies by the IMF and OECD have repeatedly highlighted weaknesses in supervision, regulation and co-operation in particular centres. Lax incorporation rules, poor customer identification and record keeping, combined with inadequate mutual assistance and information sharing arrangements are seen as providing a low risk back door to the financial system for criminals.

Since the early 2000s a lot of work has taken place in this sector. The IMF has comprehensively assessed most OFCs, and global supervisory groups such as the International Organisation of Securities Commissions (IOSCO) are monitoring compliance with international standards in each jurisdiction. However, concerns remain about a few jurisdictions, which have inadequate standards and the ability of others to remain compliant as standards evolve.

It is therefore important when dealing with companies and individuals based in an OFC to check whether the OFC is considered to be well regulated. If it is found to be a jurisdiction with a recent or current history of problems, extra care should be taken before entering into any relationship, and subsequent conduct of business should be more closely monitored.

FATF Example 15: Terrorist group uses same laundering methods as organised crime

The money laundering method of the regional liberation movement is identical to that of traditional criminal groups; first, the money is deposited into various banks of the region, where the issue of certificates of deposit takes place. Then, these certificates are deposited through intermediary companies in numbered accounts in banks at offshore tax havens, which may only be accessed by code. In the third phase, some of this money is transferred to several European banks from which cheques or payment orders are issued from differing current accounts. Finally, the money is transferred to accounts without arousing suspicion in the territory where the liberation movement is active.

Shell Banks

Shell banks are essentially banks that operate in name only in a jurisdiction where they are authorised. They have no employees or operations at the postal addresses, which are usually a PO Box or an accommodation addresses. Correspondence to these facilities is forwarded to wherever the shell bank is conducting its business at the time. There is international concern that shell banks cannot be effectively supervised and inspected. In some jurisdictions they have historically operated entirely outside the scope of regulation.

The Basel Committee for Banking Supervision (the "Basel Committee") has recommended that banks should not be allowed to maintain correspondent banking relations with shell banks in foreign jurisdictions. It is also seeking an end to shell banks by the phasing out of their licenses. In some countries it is now illegal to offer certain services to shell banks. In any event, use of a shell bank in a transaction is a reason to exercise great care.

On investigation it may prove that what was thought to be a shell bank is in fact the subsidiary of a financial institution licensed in a reputable jurisdiction and subject to effective consolidated supervision. In such cases, the rules on shell banks probably do not apply. However it is important be sure with which type of entity one is dealing and how they are viewed by the regulators.

Agents, Representatives and beneficial Owners

Good judgement and knowledge of the client's business is required to tell whether or not complex corporate structures are part of a genuine scheme, or rather lacking a readily apparent business logic. Much will depend on knowing who is ultimately in control of the entities in question and the quantity and quality of any evidence available to reach decisions.

Not all customers are acting for their own account. Sometimes an individual may be acting as an agent or representative for someone else. There is nothing wrong with this whilst it is for *bona fide* business reasons and they disclose who they are ultimately representing.

Occasionally, though, an apparently respectable customer may be providing cover for a criminal person or organisation. In many languages there is a term for this technique (e.g. acting as a "man of straw" in English or "*hombre de paja*" in Spanish) which reflects the fact that it is not always possible to establish for whom the front person is working.

When the client is a business or organisation, it is even more difficult. The contact may in fact be just an employee, though with an important job title. It may not be immediately apparent who the person or persons behind them in the business or organisation really is or are. Even where the ownership of the firm or organisation is clear, it may not always be possible to tell that it is a false front or cover and who is really benefiting from the activities being undertaken.

Though an organisation may appear to be owned, for example, by its directors, in reality it may be funded and controlled by a third party who ultimately gains advantage from the organisation's activities – a legal or natural person called a "beneficial owner".

When conducting the basic checks outlined above, particularly the client identification checks, it is important to find out whether your firm is entering into a relationship with an unknown beneficial owner who wants to use you for criminal purposes. This is an important and complex area.

In the long run it will pay to be especially careful in making sure you establish details of the ownership and control of the business or organisation in question, by obtaining the necessary documentation and recording it carefully. If a firm cannot satisfy itself that it knows with whom it is forming the business relationship, it should not enter into or continue the business relationship.

Getting a clear Statement of beneficial Ownership

It is not just good business practice to establish if a client is acting on behalf of another person. It may also be a legal requirement. One way to fulfil this duty is to ask the person with whom you are dealing to make a written statement that they act for themselves and no other, or where this is not the case, to supply in addition:

- The name of the natural person or legal person for whom they act (NB there may be more than one beneficial owner)
- The residential or business address of that person.

In both cases it is important to collect appropriate identification data on both beneficial owners and those representing them. The identification data required of beneficial owners is almost invariably the same as that required of direct owners, whether natural or legal persons. Where identification data is not produced, or is unsatisfactory, a firm should decline to continue the relationship.

Going forward

Being satisfied of a customer's identity is not something you just do once and there may even be a legal requirement to re-identify clients where there has been a long gap between transactions. If doubts arise, for example previously obtained data is found to be untrue, incomplete or out of date, clients should in any case be asked to re-identify themselves.

Clients should also be advised it is their responsibility to advise promptly of changes in identity data provided. Failure to report changes in identity data may be in itself a breach of the law or contractual relationship and thus grounds for discontinuing the relationship.

If you can no longer tell who your client is, or who really controls or beneficially owns a business, you may want to withdraw from the relationship. If there are grounds for suspicion (as opposed to finding certain aspects of a client's arrangements novel or a little unusual) you should follow your firm's procedures for reporting suspicious activity or file a suspicious activity report yourself as appropriate. In most jurisdictions you will (a) have a legal duty to do so and (b) be liable to severe penalties if you don't.

Record Keeping

Identification data collected can be recorded:

- In the contract or bill of sale documenting the business undertaken, or
- In an addendum to such documentation, or
- On a special form.

If the identification data required subsequently changes, you may need to update the contract, bill or the form accordingly.

Client identification documents, and any supporting records or copies, must be stored securely, usually for a minimum of five years and with 7 – 10 years not uncommon in some countries. They must be kept in a safe place (e.g. protected against theft, fire, and water) and in a form that allows them to be easily retrieved. It is important to bear in mind any general rules of the storage and retrieval of evidence. You will also have to abide by the relevant data protection legislation to ensure appropriate confidentiality.

A basic principle of unwinding money laundering operations is being able to "follow the money". You therefore also need to keep transaction records in such a form and in such detail as to permit the authorities to trace quickly where client money has come from, and where it has gone to, and to establish the mechanisms involved.

Keep in mind that actions may later be subject to scrutiny and that they will be judged with the benefit of hindsight. Remember to make notes of important conversations at the time they occur, especially when relying on statements made by the client which cannot be verified (e.g. future business plans) and which must therefore be taken at face value.

The importance of keeping records in a safe place

The above guidance outlines what is generally necessary in most jurisdictions. You should read the specific industry guidelines that affect your sector carefully to establish exactly when and what to record and for how long to store it.

Personal and organisational Responsibility

It is normal for a senior member of the business to be made responsible for managing the overall risk of money laundering and there may be a legal requirement to appoint a money laundering reporting officer (MLRO). If the size of the organisation allows, someone should also be appointed to make sure anti-money laundering tasks are being properly fulfilled. This person is sometimes called a compliance officer.

An important part of the compliance officer's role is to work out (or find out from other sources) how the business might be at risk from money laundering and what prevention measures can be taken. Another part is to check that cases where suspicions arise are properly handled by the MLRO.

In larger businesses there may be many compliance officers, and a separate MLRO, all reporting to a senior manager. In a small business it may be that one person has to handle all things relating to money laundering. Ideally, whoever is appointed to these positions will have some knowledge of the subject from their professional background, e.g. as a lawyer or accountant. If not, they may well need to obtain training in the necessary specialist skills.

Reporting Suspicions

Why Report?

Those with client contact are those who can best tackle money laundering at the point where it occurs. Acting responsibly where there is suspicion of money laundering is an important way to protect the economic prosperity of your business community, to keep up defences against violent extremism and to protect your organisation from being compromised by money launderers.

Making a report about irregular financial practice is neither a political denunciation nor a breach of business secrecy. It is something that can be done to alert the authorities to a situation that might get a business into problems or develop into deep trouble, such as a terrorist attack.

A number of constitutional courts have also looked at the question of secrecy and the prevention of money laundering. They have generally concluded that the rights of privacy for personal data are not unlimited where public safety is involved, and that the prevention of money laundering falls within the category of public safety.

Reporting is now accepted as being as part of the job in the key financial sectors where money laundering laws have long been in place. As employees become more familiar with clients and their businesses, so the quality of reporting has improved and those with client contact have become more experienced in spotting money laundering attempts. As money laundering regulations are applied to other sectors, so all employees in these sectors need to know their legal and social responsibilities.

Unusual Behaviour

One of the key elements of preventing money laundering is spotting unusual behaviour. The most common request from people who receive money-laundering training is for information on, and examples of, unusual behaviour.

The short answer is that unusual behaviour is whatever seems unusual in the circumstances. The more experience you have of your business sector and the more experience you have of clients, the easier it is to spot things that don't look right. You need to get know your customer, know your business and the business your customer is in, and above all to *use your initiative*.

FATF Example 16: Gold purchases facilitate laundering

An asset management company was responsible for managing the bank portfolios of two individuals active in gold purchases in Africa. The purchased African gold was then sold to a gold working company in Country F, which in turn forwarded its payments to the accounts of the sellers.

Debits were regularly made from these accounts to accounts in another European country. Desiring to verify the use of the funds, the asset management company requested its clients to provide a description of the channels used for making the payments for the gold in Africa. The information received permitted the company to identify an intermediary residing in Europe who was responsible for paying the suppliers in Country F. The individual in question was described as being closely associated with a corrupt regime in Africa.

Based on this information, the asset management company reported the case to the FIU and proceeded to block the accounts. Information exchanged with foreign counterparts permitted the linking of this illegal trade with an ongoing foreign investigation, which targeted the same individual for arms trafficking. The case was transmitted to the office of the public prosecutor which is now working with the foreign authorities to dismantle these operations.

As well as the information picked up from the client, useful information can be obtained from inquiries about normal practice in the relevant sector. The press, especially the specialist press, is a good source of current information. Background research may include walking or driving past an address to ensure it is what it claims to be or playing the " mystery shopper".

It may be that a particular transaction the client undertakes or the general way the client conducts business is unusual. A very clear sign may stand out, such as a client:

- Giving false information or documentation about a deal, an event or a company
- Making or receiving undocumented transfers from unknown sources
- Undertaking deals that make no apparent commercial sense
- Insisting on dealing with your particular organisation for subjective reasons and "leaving money on the table" for you.

Sometimes attention is aroused by less obvious developments such as a client:

- Having very good revenue without appearing to have large operating expenses
- Being very successful in an industry sector or geographic region that is otherwise run down.

Appendix 4 sets out some of the more common circumstances ("Red Flags") that should alert you to the dangers of money laundering and fraud. However, with so many possible types of business transactions, a comprehensive list of unusual behaviour is impossible. At the end of the day there is no substitute for a politely and judiciously suspicious mind applying comprehensive and clear internal procedures.

The Drive Past

Suspicious Behaviour

So when does unusual behaviour become suspicious and therefore reportable? After all, what is suspicious in one situation may be innocent in another, and simply checking against endless lists can lead people to stop following their intuition and common sense.

Your sector guidelines may emphasize certain types of Red Flag but they usually make clear that:

- By itself, one unusual example of behaviour *may or may not* be suspicious behaviour
- Taken together with other supporting observations, unusual behaviour *may well* be suspicious

The key questions are "is there a reasonable explanation for this behaviour" and "is it adequate given all the facts to hand?" You have to use your experience and judgement to ask yourself and the client the right questions. The answers will help you decide whether an unusual fact or combination of facts represents suspicious activity. If it does, then you should report it. If you are in doubt you should seek help, for example from the compliance officer or person responsible for reporting money laundering in your organisation, or from an expert adviser.

Reporting

Where you suspect money laundering is taking place, your business must alert the authorities by making a report. The main contact between your business and the authorities, the Money Laundering Reporting Officer (MLRO), usually has special responsibilities in law to make sure suspicious activity reports and associated evidence are properly processed and archived, including protecting the identity of the persons reporting and those reported.

In most firms unusual or suspicious activity is reported internally to the MLRO first. It is then up to the MLRO to investigate these transactions further and decide whether they warrant a formal suspicious activity report being made to the authorities. Where the suspicion is not so great it may be possible to submit an abbreviated routine report. Where there is evidence of a clear and substantial threat, direct contact with the authorities can usually be made by phone.

Reports are usually made in a standard reporting format set out in government or industry guidelines and filed with the authorities as soon as the suspicious circumstances come to your attention.

It is very important to bear in mind the following key points, which apply in jurisdictions that follow FATF recommendations:

- You must not under any circumstances let the person or persons mentioned in the report know or find out that they have been reported (i.e. you should not "tip off")
- A report in good faith is not a violation of trust or data protection laws
- The law protects the identity of the person making the report; you cannot be sued for making a report in good faith
- You are not required to report information obtained under certain types of professional privilege, e.g. when defending a client against a criminal charge

Action after a Report is made

The point about not letting people know you have reported them is very important. There are penalties for alerting criminals to the fact they are under suspicion (i.e.tipping off), so you should be careful about what you say, and to whom you say it.

Importantly, if you have made an adequate report in timely fashion you will have now protected yourself against possible charges of failure to report a suspicion. However, it is bad practice to make routine defensive reports simply to exclude any possible risk of prosecution, as this overloads the FIUs and defeats the point of entrusting professionals to use their judgement on when to report.

If you are not party to a suspicious transaction, but have simply observed and reported it, your involvement may now well be over. If you are party to the transaction you will normally be able to proceed with it if you do not hear back from the authorities within a certain time.

If the authorities do raise an initial objection to a transaction proceeding there may be another deadline after which the transaction may go ahead if no further objection has been raised (sometimes called a "moratorium"). The precise procedure to follow will be set out in information provided by the authority to which you make reports and in sector regulations and guidelines. Full records of the report, underlying evidence and outcome should be kept.

Good Practice Principles: KYA, KYB, KYC And KYE

Laws, regulations, guidelines and rules all help to shut the door on money laundering and terrorist financing. At the heart of them lie lessons often learned the hard way in the long and costly fight against money laundering.

These lessons are summarised in a number of basic principles that can help you avoid pitfalls that others have fallen into. They are good practice whether or not you are subject to money laundering regulation.

The principles of vigilance against money laundering are not formally defined – their scope can vary according to industry sector and country. However, in broad terms they are as follows:

Know Your Administration (KYA)
The KYA principle emphasises the need to make sure your internal procedures and documentation are reliable. It is important that you are able to collect, record and retrieve all relevant details of your anti-money laundering procedures, as well as your clients and their transactions, due diligence work, training and action taken where unusual or suspicious activity has arisen.

KYA helps you to know what decisions must be made, who must make them, the basis on which to make them and to be confident that your decisions are reasonable, timely and in line with the law. If you are subject to regulatory supervision it helps to "show you know". This adds to your own protection and also allows you to build up a long-term profile of both your own business and the type of business *bona fide* clients do.

FATF Example 17: Currency conversion conceals laundering operation

Using various identities, the resident of a neighbouring country, went on several occasions to several tellers of a branch of a bank in order to exchange the equivalent of approximately USD 11,000 into a third country currency. The banknotes presented were strangely coloured and had a bad odour as if they had been hidden and stored without protection from the environment over a long period. The Prosecutor's Office managed to block a part of the funds involved. The investigation revealed that the individual was known for, among other things, bank hold ups and armed robbery as a member of a criminal organisation, with the proceeds of these crimes being in the same currency as the banknotes presented to the bank tellers.

Know Your Business (KYB)

The KYB principle emphasises the need to understand in detail the type of transaction your business is undertaking or planning to undertake with a client. It can also extend to knowing the specific characteristics of your business as it applies to a given class of client – say, those in the import-export business.

The underlying idea is that a good knowledge of your own business lines makes it easier to spot non-standard customers and transactions, to undertake standard precautions that the situation merits and to confirm whether or not there are suspicions that need to be reported.

FATF Example 18: Underground bank launders South Asian funds

An FIU was alerted to atypical financial movements that affected bank accounts of an individual of Asian origin, into whose bank account cash was regularly deposited. The deposits, carried out by a close friend exceeded USD 2.6 million in one year. These sums were then transferred to a second account opened by the suspect in his country of origin.

Analysis of the case showed that the person in question was acting as a "banker" for the Asian community situated in several European Union countries for whom he provided cheques for cash in the currency of countries where the funds were going. The main actor in this case is suspected of masterminding a laundering scheme for proceeds of heroin trafficking controlled from abroad.

Know Your Customer (KYC)

The KYC principle is similar in that (as described in Chapter 5) it emphasises the need to identify, and confirm the identity of, a client or counterparty as well as to build up a general picture of their business. As ever, the idea is to become familiar with the client's activities and pattern of business over time. This is as a basis for spotting unusual or unexpected developments and changes that might confirm or exclude the suspicion of money laundering. Over time, and by comparing the activities of clients, you may also be able to build up an idea of what is usual in your client's business sectors.

FATF Example 19: TF laundering through diamond sector funds

The FIU of Country F received several disclosures from different banks concerning two persons as well as one company active in the diamond trade. The persons were account holders at these banks. In the space of a few months the accounts of these different clients showed a great number of fund transfers to and from foreign countries. Moreover a little while after the opening of his account one of the clients collected several bank cheques in dollars for significant amounts.

According to the financial information obtained by the FIU, it appeared that one of the accounts of the company was credited with significant amounts of dollars originating from companies active in the diamond industry and debited with several transfers to the Middle

East in favour of a European citizen born in Africa and residing in the Middle East.

One of the directors of the company, a citizen of Country F residing in Africa, held an account at a bank also in Country F to which several transfers took place to and from foreign countries (Europe, Africa, North America, the Middle East). The transfers from foreign countries mainly took place in dollars and were then converted to the local currency to process transfers to foreign countries on the one hand, and to accounts in Country F belonging to the client and his wife on the other hand. According to information collected by the FIU, it appeared that the prosecutor had opened a file related to trafficking in diamonds originating from Africa.

The important transfers of funds by the company trading in diamonds were mainly destined to the same person residing in the Middle East. Police sources revealed that this person as well as the client who had cashed the cheques was suspected of having bought diamonds from the rebel army of an African country and of having smuggled them into Country F on behalf of a terrorist organisation. Moreover, it appeared that certain persons and companies linked with the aforementioned clients have already been reported by the FIU in other files for money laundering derived from organised crime.

Know Your Employee (KYE)

Some people add a fourth principle – Know Your Employee (KYE). Ineffective, untrained and dishonest employees are a weak spot in your defences. If, for whatever reason, company employees (from top to bottom) do not follow the KYC and KYB principles then these defences are breached and the company is at risk.

It is as important to check on the identity of an employee as it is to check on a client. The same types of precautions need to be undertaken, especially reference checks and checks that the employee is not using a stolen identity. These checks need to be made at the time of first hiring and also during employment. The greater an employee's access to account opening and funds transfer systems, the more detailed and frequent checks should to be.

FATF Example 20: Retail gold purchases serve as direct method of laundering

A foreign national used the services of a bureau de change to buy 265 ingots of gold with a total value of about USD 2,440,000, paid in cash. These transactions took place over a period of 18 months. The buyer, who did not have a bank account, alternated temporary jobs with periods of unemployment, suggesting that he was acting on behalf of a third party, whether a natural or legal person, who was probably involved in drug trafficking. The facts were forwarded to the prosecutor, and an investigation is ongoing.

At all Times, in all Places

Whether legally obliged to or not, it is worth taking time to think about these four principles and how they might apply to your own business area. Following, adapting and developing them in line with relevant rules and guidelines, with outside help if necessary, is a sure way of establishing safe working methods. It should also help advance the businesses concerned.

Staying alert

Every business should take steps to stay informed about the risks of money laundering and how to prevent them from materialising. Constant awareness and thinking about the purpose and nature of normal client relationships is required to spot situations which don't make sense and where extra care may be necessary.

Remember to make all the use you can of local and national trade association or government information, and information from open sources like the World Wide Web, if you have access. You may also want to compare experiences with your friends and friendly competitors. Again, the case studies and sources of help in the Appendices are designed to help you with awareness training.

The points that have been made so far in this guide are not meant

Sleeping safe in the knowledge…

to scare you or put you off from doing business. They are simply meant to draw your attention to the fact that, like shoplifting, theft, fraud or physical attacks on goods and staff, money laundering is a real threat. It must and can be taken seriously by following a common sense approach, staying alert and bearing in mind the appropriate codes of conduct.

If you do not have to follow specific governmental regulations you might still want to consider how guidelines intended for other areas could nonetheless protect your business. For example, you might use them as a base for your own voluntary code to help everyone in your business be aware of money laundering risks and how to avoid them.

If this is done you will find that your risks of being abused by money launderers are much reduced − it will be easier for them to target those less prepared than you.

SEVEN

Sector Considerations

In the regulated sectors of economically advanced countries there are plenty of source materials with detailed explanations of anti-money laundering risks and country-specific responses for the specialist to consult. This section is intended to provide an overview of key money laundering issues as they apply more generally to the major business sectors across the world, as a background to further reading and as a guide to self-help in areas where anti-money laundering systems are not so well developed.

Banking

"Banks are our first line of defence against money launderers, drug dealers and even terrorists who would attempt to abuse our financial institutions. Banks that disregard their duty to conduct adequate due diligence and report suspicious financial activities allow themselves to be exploited for criminal purposes."

Michael Chertoff

The banking system is especially vulnerable to attempts at money laundering because of the opportunities offered if its protective barriers can be breached. Once launderers are accepted into the system, criminal and terrorist funds, especially cash, can be moved quickly from place to place in different sizes, currencies and financial instruments. Know Your Customer ("KYC"), in terms of both initial identification and ongoing awareness of their transaction patterns, is central to the integrity of the banking system. It also underpins the key role of banks in the prevention, detection and reporting of money laundering.

"Is it <u>where</u> I've parked my car or what I've got parked <u>in</u> my car, Officer?

Nowadays banks have particular problems in the identification of customers, in that they may not have face-to-face contact with the customer or the account beneficiary. They may be dealing through third parties such as correspondent banks, financial intermediaries, trust companies, lawyers or accountants. They may obtain customers through the internet. Monitoring transactions may also be difficult in areas such as private banking where customers value confidentiality.

Banks are also vulnerable simply because the services they offer are essential to criminals. Drug bosses need their fortunes managed, just as an honest person needs a savings account. Terrorists need their funds transferred, just as a student living away from home may need cash wired from time to time. Inevitably, banks will be tried out by a few dishonest customers, as well as the many honest ones.

Where large sums are involved, investment and commercial banking services are particularly attractive because they routinely process high value amounts. Correspondent banking relationships[1] ease electronic transfer of title to financial assets between accounts in various parts of the world. If a trading account can be opened with a securities firm, it can be used to effect trades (real or fictitious) creating nominal profits and losses that can then be settled internationally through the normal clearance and settlements systems. If the financial institution is in a jurisdiction with lax controls and a record for non co-operation in anti-money laundering matters, then so much the better.

FATF Example 21: Non-resident bank accounts move money offshore

In one European country (Country A), transactions involving non-residential accounts of companies from off–shore areas can be divided in two groups according to the form of the account and the technique used, as follows: (1) cash operations in connection with non-residential accounts and (2) cashless operations on non-residential accounts.

As regards cash operations through non-residential accounts, the FIU in Country A had a recent case which dealt with two companies registered in two other European countries. Foreign citizens, who were authorised to represent the companies, opened non-residential accounts at two Country A banks. Over a period of 20 months, cash was deposited in these accounts totalling over USD 8,000,000. Later they brought cash from abroad and avoided reporting requirements in Country A. Generally, the cash was in small denomination bank notes. As soon as the cash was deposited, they gave an order to the bank for the transfer of money to the credit of numerous foreign companies registered in five other countries. The legal basis for these transactions consisted of invoices from companies engaged in the selling of tobacco products and alcohol that were issued for the payment of large quantities of cigarettes.

In connection with these transactions, the Country A's FIU found that the money originated from tax fraud against European Union interests and from the smuggling of cigarettes. With the help of forged documentation, the perpetrators misrepresented to Country A's customs authorities that the cigarettes were exported from European Union countries to the East. In fact, the cigarettes were sold on the black market in several European countries. Non-residential accounts were opened in Country A with the single purpose of laundering the illegal funds derived from the sale of smuggled cigarettes. Deposits into the accounts of off-shore companies were made in an attempt to cover up the real origins of the money, to remove links with the perpetrators of the predicate offences and also to cover payment for new quantities of cigarettes.

Basel Committee for Banking Supervision

The principal international standards body for banks, the Basel Committee, issued guidance in October 2001 to the effect that banks must have clear customer acceptance, customer identification, account monitoring and risk monitoring procedures. The guidance includes giving special attention to high risk accounts and clients accepted on the basis of identification procedures conducted by third parties, such as correspondent banks.

In particular, the recommendations state that:

- Senior management should sign off on the acceptance of high risk customers
- Extra care should be taken with private clients and special procedures established to identify and manage the affairs of politically exposed persons
- Special rules should be followed when accepting business through introducers, to ensure there is no compromise with regard to due diligence standards, procedures or systems, and to enable both verification of the introducer's due diligence and inspection of supporting files
- Similar due diligence is required with regard to correspondent banks

- Relationships with shell banks or banks in jurisdictions where AML procedures are lax should be brought to an end
- The principles of KYC must be applied in a consistent way across global banking groups.

Work by the Basel Committee since August 2003 has emphasised how banks should not set customer due diligence (CDD) standards by reference to the legal minimum but more broadly and at a level which allows risks to be identified, monitored and mitigated (see Appendix 2 for details of where the Basel Recommendations can be found).

FATF Example 22: A terrorist organisation uses wire transfers to move money to further its activities across borders

A terrorist organisation in Country X was observed using wire transfers to move money in Country Y that was eventually used for paying rent for safe houses, buying and selling vehicles, and purchasing electronic components with which to construct explosive devices. The organisation used "bridge" or "conduit" accounts in Country X as a means of moving funds between countries. The accounts at both ends were opened in the names of people with no apparent association with the structure of terrorist organisation but who were linked to one another by kinship or similar ties. There were thus the apparent family connections that could provide a justification for the transfers between them if necessary.

Funds, mainly in the form of cash deposits by the terrorist organisation were deposited into bank accounts from which the transfers are made. Once the money was received at the destination, the holder either left it on deposit or invested it in mutual funds where it remained hidden and available for the organisation's future needs. Alternatively, the money was transferred to other bank accounts managed by the organisation's correspondent financial manager, from where it was distributed to pay for the purchase of equipment and material or to cover other ad hoc expenses incurred by the organisation in its clandestine activities.

The Basel Committee's recommendations have been reinforced by the revised FATF 40 Recommendations. These stipulate that national anti-money laundering regulations on cross border correspondent banking should require financial institutions, in addition to normal due diligence, to:

- Evaluate fully a correspondent bank's business, its reputation and supervision record as well as any history of involvement in money laundering
- Document what each institution has to do to prevent money laundering
- Adopt special measures for "payable through accounts" to make sure the correspondent bank performs verification and ongoing due diligence of clients with direct access to correspondent bank accounts and the ability to provide customer identification data on request
- Assess its anti-money laundering terrorist financing measures
- Get senior management approval for new correspondent banking relationships.

IOSCO and the Securities Markets

In the securities markets, IOSCO, the International Organisation of Securities Commissions, works on a thematic basis. Since its 1992 Technical Committee's Report on Money Laundering, it has also made reports and resolutions on a number of topics related to money laundering. These include:

- Beneficial ownership
- Customer identification
- Record keeping
- Collection of Information
- Mutual Co-operation

FATF Example 23: Stockbroker accepts criminal funds in cash

A stockbroker in Country C continuously accepted cash deposits from a client in the range of USD 7,000 to USD 18,000. The funds were placed in the money market fund of the client's sister and withdrawn through the issuance of cheques. After the broker was arrested on unrelated embezzlement charges, the client's identity became known to law enforcement. When the police conducted a background check on the client, it was revealed that the stockbroker's client was a known drug dealer.

In its Objectives and Principles of Securities Legislation (1998 and 2002) IOSCO stresses the role of local regulators in determining what anti-money laundering policies and procedures should be put in place. Its May 2004 Guidance Note on Principles of Client Identification and Beneficial Ownership for the Securities Industry interprets the FATF Revised 40 and Special IX Recommendations for use in securities, futures and leveraged foreign exchange businesses.

Getting senior management approval for new relationships

A key feature of the securities sector is that transactions often take place against a background of fast moving markets. It is accepted therefore that in some cases verification of client identity may only be possible after a trade has been executed. However, the elements of identification should be in place and if problems in securing adequate client identification are subsequently encountered then the trade must be unwound.

FATF Example 24: Fraud money invested in securities market

A brokerage firm opened several accounts for a group of twelve linked individuals, including a non-resident account that was used to record very large movements and apparently to centralise most of the suspected flows, which totalled more than USD 18 million.
The launderers used the following two mechanisms:

- the accounts of some of the parties involved were credited with large sums received from countries of concern, which were invested in the stocks of listed companies in Country W; and
- the accounts of the individuals concerned were credited with sums from regions of concern, which were transferred to the non-resident account (the first accounts were used as screens).

This securities buy/sell mechanism was used to filter the flows through the broker and subsequently the clearer and custodian. Once filtered, the funds were sent to locations in regions of concern and offshore financial centres.

This information showed that the co-opted broker had been used to launder the proceeds from various forms of frauds. The manager of the brokerage firm served as a relay for the criminal organisations involved.

Later that year the investigators engaged in a series of co-ordinated searches. Three subjects were arrested and charged for failure to register as a financial business and approximately USD 60,000 in cash and cheques were seized. Additionally, a bank account was identified containing approximately USD 130,000 which was used to facilitate the illegal wire transfers to destinations outside Country A. The subjects are currently awaiting trial.

Private Banking and the Wolfsberg Group

A set of client due diligence standards for private banking has been drawn up by the Wolfsberg Group, an association of 12 global banks first established in 2000. However, the standards are not mandatory and act only as guidelines. Private banking operations must first and foremost abide by the money laundering regulations of the countries whose jurisdiction they fall under by virtue of their operations.

The Wolfsberg Group's recommendations and guidance cover the same issues as many countries' regulations but focus on beneficial ownership, client identity, intermediaries and Politically Exposed Persons. They stress the personal role of the private banker in ensuring proper identification, monitoring and record keeping, and the responsibility of the organisation to have proper arrangements, controls and audits.

The Group maintains a website on money laundering issues that includes useful information on CDD in private banking in the form of answers to frequently asked questions. It also has links to a commercial due diligence data repository and from there to the ICC's Financial Investigation Bureau (see Appendix 2).

In establishing and ensuring the effectiveness of anti-money laundering systems, senior managers should monitor anti-money laundering activity and make it known that high standards of commitment are expected at all levels. It is also important for senior management to ensure systems are tested where this is mandatory or indicated by risk analysis.

Simple IT systems can help by making better use of the large amounts of information typically kept by banks. Sharing information across product and geographical areas helps with client ID. It can also help to ensure anti-money laundering standards are consistent across a bank's operations in countries with different anti-money laundering regimes. More expensive systems allow banks to monitor high volumes of transactions and detect patterns of unusual or suspicious behaviour. The expense can be offset by combining screening with routine and specially targeted anti fraud activity.

Electronic monitoring is just one method of sampling for suspicious transactions. Other methods include selecting transactions at random or by a specific combination of criteria (e.g. size, product, country), or based on the banker's personal experience. None of this is possible however if the bank does not have the right knowledge, skills and motivation. Training at the appropriate level of detail is thus important at all levels of the bank.

Insurance

The attraction of the insurance industry to money launderers is similar to that of the banking sector: it can be manipulated into providing an easy passage of illicit funds through the financial system. FATF has recently highlighted the money laundering risks that exist across the insurance industry, and not just in the life and investment setors where regulation has previously focussed.

Insurance is a global industry with many different types of cash flows and currencies handled on a daily basis. An estimated $3 trillion is paid in insurance premia alone every year. Once in the insurance system, money can be moved around rapidly with all the appearance of legitimacy.

In particular the insurance market offers launderers:

- Different product areas (e.g. accident, life, reinsurance) with different transaction profiles. They range from routine fixed annual cash flow products to high value investment-style products such as single premium annuities and unit linked policies
- A source of funds that arouses few suspicions with banks
- Relative anonymity in volume, especially computer-marketed, sales

- A distribution chain where companies offering products do not always have control over sales by brokers or intermediaries
- Potential confusion over who is the customer – the policy holder or the beneficiary?
- The possibility to use insurance policies as transferable instruments, e.g. as collateral for loans.

FATF Example 25: An Insurance policy used to launder money

A money launderer purchased marine property and casualty insurance for a phantom ocean-going vessel. He paid large premiums on the policy and suborned the intermediaries so that frequent claims were made and paid. However, he was very careful to ensure that the claims were less than the premium payments, so that the insurer enjoyed a reasonable profit on the policy.

In this way, the money launderer was able to receive claims cheques that could be used to launder funds. The funds appeared to come from a reputable insurance company, and few questioned the source of the funds having seen the name of the company on the cheque or wire transfer.

The view, held until relatively recently, that the life insurance sector was most at risk from money laundering was based on experiences gained from investigations such as *Operation Capstone* in which US, Colombian, UK and Isle of Man investigators exposed $80 million of money laundering by Colombian drug traffickers.

Operation Capstone revealed that Colombian cartels were obtaining life insurance policies using a small number of insurance brokers. The cartel was named (using front men) as beneficiary and the policies were purchased using the proceeds of drug dealing. The premia were transmitted electronically or sent by cheques drawn by third parties. To obtain "legitimate" proceeds, the cartels were simply redeeming their policies early, despite the hefty discount they had to accept in the process. The following example includes variations on this theme.

FATF Example 26: Money Launderers use the insurance industry to clean their funds

Clients in several countries used the services of an intermediary to purchase insurance policies. Identification was taken from the client by way of an ID card, but these details were unable to be clarified by the providing institution locally, which relied on the due diligence checks of the intermediary.

The policy was put in place and the relevant payments made by the intermediary to the local institution. Then, after a couple of months had elapsed, the institution would receive notification from the client stating that there was now a change in circumstances, they would have to close the policy incurring the losses, and would thus request a reimbursement (by cheque).

On other occasions the policy would be left to run for a couple of years before being closed with the request that the payment be made to a third party. This reimbursement cheque was then often processed by the local financial institution without further question since the payment came from another reputable local institution.

Life business does not have to involve single premium business to be risky. Top-ups to existing life assurance and pension plans can also provide a means of placing proceeds of crime. With imagination and intent, most forms of insurance can be abused to serve as laundering instruments, and not just products with an investment or resale value.

Recent studies show that general insurance and reinsurance sectors also have their weaknesses. This is all the more true where money laundering follows fraud, which makes it doubly important for insurers and those who sell their products to be on their guard.

FATF Example 27: Money laundering following insurance firm pay outs

Police in Country A uncovered a case of trafficking in stolen cars where the perpetrators provoked accidents in Country B to be able to claim the damages. The proceeds were laundered via public works companies. A network consisting of two teams operated in two different regions of Country A. Luxury vehicles were stolen and given false number plates before being taken to Country B. An insurance contract was taken out in the first country on these vehicles. In Country B, the vehicles were deliberately written off and junk vehicles with false number plates were bought using false identity documents to be able to claim the damages from the insurance firms in Country A.

Around a hundred luxury stolen vehicles were used in this scheme to claim the damages resulting from the simulated or intentional accidents that were then fraudulently declared to the insurance firms. The total loss was over USD 2.5 million. The country in which the accidents occurred was chosen because its national legislation provided for prompt payment of damages.

On receipt of the damages, the false claimants gave 50% of the sum in cash to the leader of the gang who invested these sums in Country B. The investigations uncovered bank transfers amounting to over USD 12,500 per month from the leader's accounts to the country in question. The money was invested in the purchase of numerous public works vehicles and in setting up companies in this sector in Country B. Investigations also revealed that the leader of the gang had a warehouse in which luxury vehicles used for his trafficking operation were stored. It was also established that there was a business relationship between the leader and a local property developer, suggesting that the network sought to place part of its gains into real estate.

Legally speaking, the roles played in the insurance sector, e.g. broker, introducer, insurer, reinsurer, underwriter – as well as the type and geographic location of the client – will govern the anti-money laundering arrangements required. The arrangements will also depend on factors, such as:

- the type of insurance the client wishes to obtain compared with the nature of their lifestyle or business
- the number and significance of the transactions involved
- whether the counterparty is regulated and where.

In practical terms, you are best advised to identify your counterparties immediately in all circumstances. By the time any benefits are likely to be paid out you should know who the client is and who, too, is the beneficiary. Each insurance product, as well as each and any associated premium and benefit, is best seen as an individual transaction. In many countries the law requires this.

However, the insurance sector does have areas of business where relationships may be established before identities are verified. The International Association of Insurance Supervisors (IAIS) points out that where this occurs (e.g. group pensions schemes, pledging of policies as collateral) tight controls are necessary on the extent of business that can be conducted until the relevant identities are established which, as mentioned, must occur before any rights are exercised under the policy. Steps taken to verify the identity of clients who are not seen face-to-face may need to include supplementary measures so as to mitigate the higher risks associated with such business[2].

As with other sectors, simplified CDD measures are in order where transactions are of:

- low value (for example a yearly life premium below USD/EUR 1,000 or a single premium of USD/EUR 2,500 or below)
- low risk (policies with no surrender clause or collateral value, non-contributory pension plans, government business).

Similarly, greater attention should be given to complex, high value one-off transactions where the risk may not be readily apparent.

In addition to following "Know Your Business" and "Know Your Customer" principles, it is also important to remember "Know Your Employee". By placing a person on the inside of a broker or insurance firm, a money laundering organisation can ensure that client identification procedures are relaxed or the results altered, and the same with suspicious transaction reporting. Likewise it is important to check that key employees and intermediary agents are who they say they are, and that they do not get drawn into such conspiracies.

FATF Example 28: Drug trafficker launders funds through purchase of life insurance policy

A person (later arrested for drug trafficking) made a financial investment (life insurance) of USD 250,000 by means of an insurance broker. He contacted an insurance broker and delivered a total amount of USD 250,000 in three cash instalments. The insurance broker did not report the delivery of that amount and deposited the three instalments in the bank. These actions raised no suspicion at the bank, since the insurance broker was known to be connected to the insurance sector. The insurance broker later delivered to the insurance company responsible for making the financial investment, three cheques from a bank account under his name totalling USD 250,000, thus avoiding raising any suspicions with the insurance company.

The IAIS has published guidance stressing the importance of underwriting checks and of CDD activity along similar lines to that recommended in other parts of the financial sector. In particular it stresses the need for attention to:

- Identifying the underlying principal (as opposed to the policy holder)
- The relationship between underwriters, loss adjusters and claims investigators
- Special training for staff in high-risk areas.

IAIS's Insurance Core Principles and Methodology (October 2003) contains updated core principles for insurance supervision and under Core Principle 28, the requirements of the FATF Revised 40 and Special IX Recommendations must be met for supervision to meet IAIS standards.

IAIS has also issued Guidance Paper No. 5 (October 2004), which sets out how international money laundering standards should apply in the insurance sector. The scope of this document goes beyond the life and investment related insurance activities that have traditionally been subject to regulation to include the new areas of concern, where regulation has a shorter history.

Like national financial supervisors, IAIS sets out a risk-based approach to anti-money laundering. In addition to products already mentioned, areas of risk highlighted in the 2004 Guidance Paper and identified by FATF in its 2004 Typologies Exercise include:

- Early redemption features
- Bearer policies
- Fixed and variable annuities
- Assignment of policies and claims (including viatical deals)
- Overpayment of premia
- Abuse of cooling off periods
- Third party premia payments
- Payouts overseas
- Fictitious companies
- New technology

Both FATF and IAIS stress the importance of CDD and of checking the reliability of CDD performed by intermediaries. The guidance and the 2004 FATF Typologies report on risk in the insurance sector are recommended reading (see Appendix 2). Importantly, the guidance points out that CDD is an ongoing requirement, and also provide good examples of the type of event that trigger detailed or repeat CDD. Conversely, it highlights areas of lower risk where simplified CDD is indicated. In either case, unsatisfactory outcomes entail the termination of the relationship.

Responsibilities, duties to have arrangements, training, record keeping and suspicious transaction reporting procedures in this sector follow the lines set out in Chapter 6. IAIS stresses the need for effective monitoring of both business and money laundering risk management arrangements, including making sure that foreign branches and subsidiaries comply with "home" standards. Appendix 4 lists "Red Flags" that warn of possible misuse of the insurance sector, based on research by IAIS and other sources.

FATF Example 29: Criminal funds laundered through payment of insurance premiums

A company director from Company W, Mr. H, set up a money laundering scheme involving two companies, each one established under two different legal systems. Both of the entities were to provide financial services and financial guarantees and he would act as director.

These companies wired the sum of USD 1.1 million to the accounts of Mr. H in Country S. It is likely that the funds originated in some sort of criminal activity and had already been introduced in some way into the financial system. Mr. H also received transfers from Country C.

Funds were transferred from one account to another (several types of accounts were involved, including both current and savings accounts). Through one of these transfers, the funds were transferred to Country U from a current account in order to make payments on life insurance policies. The investment in these policies was the main mechanism in the scheme for laundering the funds. The premiums paid for the life insurance policies in Country U amounted to some USD 1.2 million and represented the last step in the laundering operation.

IAIS Guidance Paper No. 10 (October 2005) also provides useful insights into risk in general from the supervisor's perspective, which are of special relevance to senior management of insurance firms.

Money Transmission Services (MTS) and Foreign Exchange (FX) Bureaux

Businesses in this sector offer some of the core cash handling, currency and transfer services offered by fully-fledged banks. In contrast to banks, customers do not need to establish an ongoing relationship, and business is conducted on a transaction by transaction basis. Cash is mostly involved, but some firms offer facilities for cheques and money orders to be cashed or issued.

Money transmission is very important in some spheres of the economy, for example where migrant workers need to send money home to support their families. Foreign exchange bureaux business grew in proportion to the boom in international travel in the second half of the 20th Century.

The ability to transform cash into assets in a different form and a different place is of fundamental interest to money launderers. These businesses are thus a target both for channelling an individual transaction as well as for being run as a cover for wider scale operations. For example, an MTS might be asked to wire the countervalue of a large single amount of cash in several smaller amounts just below the relevant reporting thresholds to various banks worldwide. Likewise, the smaller cash proceeds of drug dealing at street level might be entered into the books of a phoney MTS or FX operation as routine cash handling transactions, then banked and credited to a collection account for paying away later.

Though there were always concerns that these businesses represented a weak spot for money laundering it is only recently that they have come under close scrutiny. The revised FATF 40 Recommendations clearly include both types of entity as financial institutions (see Appendix 1) and in most countries they are now subject to registration and inspection requirements, and have the same basic money laundering prevention duties and obligations as banks themselves. They may also have obligations to disclose details of agency arrangements and expected turnover.

Businesses need to be careful that their activities do not

inadvertently fall within the scope of MTS and FX bureaux. A good example of a potential problem area is the hotel that offers FX facilities or a pawnbroker that cashes checques for a regular customer. However, regulations normally provide that businesses can undertake transactions for clients provided they remain below a time and/or a value threshold.

FATF Example 30: MTS supports operations of a terrorist group

A recent successful money laundering investigation concerning a bureau de change operation uncovered evidence of the laundering of terrorist funds, derived from international smuggling. Certain similarities existed with the hawala system in that there were substantial cash payments into the bureau de change which were reflected neither in its principal books, nor its records, nor in the bureau de change's bank account. The bureau de change held a huge cash reserve, which was drawn upon when necessary by members of the terrorist organisation. In addition, the bureau de change would remit payments from its legitimate bank account to entities in other jurisdictions, on behalf of the terrorist organisation, which upon investigation was shown to be payment for contraband.

Following the guidance set out above, especially that for banks, and the Red Flags (Appendix 4) will help guard against the major risks faced by legitimate businesses. However, as discussed in the next section, not all MTS are licensed. In many countries this makes them illegal and funds deposited with them are not insured under any deposit protections schemes that may operate. Deposits with an MTS risk being stolen, or seized by the authorities, e.g. if transported illegally, e.g. across a border. The illegal MTS is in reality a form of alternative remittance system.

Alternative Remittance Systems

Not all transfers of money or value pass through the formal financial system. In some areas of the world, alternative remittance systems (ARS) are both legal and commonly used to make transfers domestically and internationally. Such payments may be in respect of personal or business matters. As these systems sometimes involve transfers of, or transformation into, non-monetary goods, they are also called informal value transfer systems (IVTS) as well as informal funds transfer systems (IFTS).

A number of terms are commonly used to describe ARS, such as "parallel", "underground" or "hawala" banking[3]. There is a long history of ARS in the Middle East and Asia and they are sometimes referred to (with spurious accuracy) as Chip Shop, Fei-Ch'ien, Hui Kuan, Hundi, Padala, Phei Kwan and, in Latin America, the Black Market Peso.

While ARS are used for legitimate transfers, their anonymity and minimal documentation standards make them vulnerable to abuse for illegal activities. In the wake of the 9/11 tragedy, ARS were widely held to play a role in financing terrorism.

FATF Example 31: Wire transfers are used as part of a terrorist fundraising campaign

An investigation in Country A of Company Z, a company thought to be involved in the smuggling and distribution of pseudoephedrine (a suspected source of revenue for terrorist organisations), revealed that employees of Company Z were sending a large number of negotiable cheques to Country B. Additional evidence revealed that the target business was acting as an unlicensed money remitter. Based on the above information, search warrants were obtained for the Company Z premises and two residences. Analysis of the documents and bank records seized as a result of the search warrants indicated that the suspects had wire transferred money to an individual with suspected ties to a terrorist group.

The most common use of ARS is by emigrant workers from India, Pakistan, the Far East, Africa and Eastern Europe living in developed countries to send money to their families. ARS have flourished because they meet a demand for accessible and efficient payments services which national and international banking systems do not provide. It has been argued[4] that poor national economic policy and financial development, together with an unstable political and security environment, encourage ARS to prosper.

ARS are built on informal procedures and trust rather than formal rules and documentation and have distinct advantages for the users. In particular they are:

- Less risky than having to transport cash personally over long distances and less expensive than professional cash couriers
- A convenient means of avoiding formal (taxes) and informal (bribes for corrupt officials) charges on cash transfers
- Quicker than bank-based alternatives, especially in remote areas
- Close and readily accessible – they do not require users to hold bank accounts
- Based on minimal documentation and accounting requirements – kinship, ethnic ties and personal relations offer greater user-friendliness and trustworthiness
- Able to grant credit/cash advance facilities
- Able to protect users from exposure to /contact with banks and other agents, which might be sensitive for cultural, religious or social reasons.
- Importantly, cheaper than commercial banks

ARS transactions are run through middlemen, who are often businessmen with wide family or trading networks. The theoretical mechanism is very old – similar to parallel payments systems that existed in 16th Century Europe – with middlemen making a book entry on accepting deposits and providing a code for the depositor to pass on to the end recipient. The end recipient then presents the code to a local middleman and obtains the money. At suitable intervals the

The Chip Shop – an alternative remittance system...

middlemen settle up between themselves, possibly taking into account other bilateral trade in goods and any offset business involving third parties.

In practice modern ARS are much more complex and use the latest technology. The system is too complex to run without records and there are clearing houses in leading European, Middle East and Asian trading centres to facilitate the settlement of accounts. The scale of operations is such that there are macroeconomic arguments for the regulation of ARS, which relate to their role in facilitating capital flight, lowering tax revenues as well as distorting trade statistics, money supply and cash in circulation figures.

However, in terms of the fight against money laundering, concerns centre on the fact that accessing the records of ARS is difficult, if not impossible. By their nature, they are low profile networks with anonymity a key service feature.

The belief that ARS are vulnerable to abuse by money launderers is based on a substantial body of evidence from investigations into cocaine, heroin and gold smuggling. Their potential for use in terrorist financing was established by investigations in the wake of the 9/11 attacks into transfers between religious charities and militant organisations. A middleman was identified as the financier in the 1998 attacks on the American embassies in Kenya and Tanzania. Six Jammu Kashmir Islamic Front (JKIF) terrorists were arrested in India in 2001 in an investigation which revealed a web of hawala institutions in Delhi, despite an earlier clamp down by the government on these institutions.

Many countries have now brought ARS within the scope of regulation in line with FATF recommendations. These recommendations are meant to ensure ARS are subject to the same controls, enforcement and sanctions procedures as conventional financial institutions. They require registration (of both the system and its individual agents) or licensing of ARS. However, because countries have different legal and economic systems, the rules in one country may well differ from those in another.

When using such systems for legal purposes, such as sending money to areas where there are few (if any) banks, it is therefore important to know whether such use is legal in all jurisdictions involved. Given that foreign exchange dealings are subject to controls (in all cases or above a certain level) in many countries, all usage of ARS should be regarded as potentially illegal.

It may also be possible for a business to become unintentionally involved in an ARS, for example by being asked to pay an amount to, or receive one from, a third party. False invoicing can also play a significant role in ARS transfers with the manipulation by ARS middlemen of sales and purchase invoice amounts in their underlying businesses an established means of disguising money flows. A person may also be asked to deliver a package of papers on a journey abroad, in return for an outstanding invoice or loan being "forgotten". All these aspects can lead to serious problems for those using the system when it comes to an investigation.

Likewise, a financial institution may become involved in collecting and transferring ARS payments flowing through an established business account. Interpol, the international police organisation and FinCEN, the US regulator, have identified transaction patterns that may indicate such use, namely:

- Significant, sometimes sudden, deposit activity in the form of cash and checks
- Payers are from one or more ethnic minority community associated with the middlemen
- Checks are payable to the primary account holder, or some secondary entity (often outside the country) somehow associated with the account
- Checks may also have some sort of notation, consisting of a name or something supposedly 'bought' with the money
- Deposit of third party checks
- Subsequent transfers to international money transmitters or purchase of negotiable instruments
- Accounts almost always show outgoing transfers to a major financial centre thought to host ARS clearing houses (e.g. Great Britain, Switzerland, and the UAE).

Accountants may also notice separate books of account, tiered profit structures for similar transactions and sales and purchase invoices involving atypical counterparties for the type of business. Interpol suggests that certain businesses are more likely to be involved in ARS. They include:

- Import/export
- Travel and related services
- Jewellery (gold, precious stones)

- Foreign exchange
- Rugs/carpets
- Used cars
- Car rentals (usually non-chain or franchise)
- Telephones/pagers

For further sources of information on ARS see Appendix 2.

Gaming

Like other gateways to the financial system, gaming in its various forms has always been a target for money launderers. The inherent risk of gaming operations is their capacity to turn "illegal" stake money into "legal" winnings by means of a bet. Historically, the aspects of risk for legitimate gaming operations are:

- Use of cash, either directly or via the purchase of betting tokens
- Lack of knowledge about the origin of stake money
- Lack of knowledge about the player
- Lack of knowledge about the true recipient of winnings
- Internet gambling

FATF Example 32: Laundering related to securities law violations and possible link with terrorism

The FIU of Country L received an initial report from a casino regarding a Mr. N, of foreign origin and residing in Western Europe, who was purchasing gaming chips using various foreign currencies in large sums. Several similar reports from other casinos regarding the same individual were then followed up.

During the same period a bank made a report about one of its customers. The bank's suspicions had been aroused by the fact that this customer (Mr. K) was the principal shareholder of Company A, whose stock had been de-listed by a major stock exchange. Company

Off-shore casinos attracting unwelcome attention

A did not have an account with this bank, but Mr. K had signature authority on an account opened in the name of offshore Company B. This account was very active: several large transfers had been made from various companies in the goods haulage sector; these funds had then been transferred in particular to an account in a tax haven in the name of another party (Mr. E). Some time later, Mr. K approached a lawyer representing the offshore Company B to ask for a bank account to be opened in the name of a Company C incorporated under a foreign legal system, whose shareholders were Mr. K and the offshore Company B. The bank refused to open this account.

Company A, whose shares were quoted on a major stock exchange, was active in the transportation of second-hand vehicles from Europe to Africa. This company, operating via Country L, has its registered office in an offshore centre. Information gathered by the FIU in Country L revealed that a stock exchange regulator had published an official notice announcing that the shares of Company A had been suspended pending an enquiry into fraudulent accounting practices at the company. These practices involved recourse to a network of offshore companies and consisted of intentionally spreading misleading information about its shares with the aim of manipulating the price. The stock market regulator has now begun a procedure to de-list this share.

From the FIU's analysis it appears that the parties appearing in this file used the financial system to conceal funds linked to stock exchange offences committed on the shares of Company A.

It appears that Mr. N, the beneficiary of the gift of several million dollars from Mr. K (principal shareholder of Company A), is the financial director of Company A. The latter had placed these funds in a share portfolio in his own name and had asked the bank if he could withdraw them in cash. The fact that the report from the bank was made before the funds were withdrawn in cash allowed the FIU to temporarily block the operation for 24 hours. This file was then urgently passed on to the public prosecutor to have seized the funds blocked following the Unit's intervention.

...It turned out incidentally that the lawyer involved in this file was already known to the police for his involvement in tax frauds carried out by means of debt-collecting agencies. Information recently collected revealed that Mr. E is also connected with Company A and is suspected by the judicial authorities of being involved in arms trafficking organised from an offshore centre where the registered office of Company A is located. What is more, there are suspicions regarding possible links between this arms trafficking and a terrorist network, the offshore centre in question being regarded as one of the bastions of this particular terrorist group.

Gaming businesses thus run very similar risks to other businesses of becoming unwittingly involved in money laundering and terrorist financing. As finally formally acknowledged by their inclusion in

FATF's Revised 40 recommendations, gaming operations function in a way analogous to some financial services, for example speculation in stocks and shares. They thus invite analogous regulation.

Even before FATF acted in June 2003, various jurisdictions sought to limit gaming and betting either entirely or by licensing operators, restricting the type and extent of games that can be played, or by rules to protect players. Historically, regulation of gaming has been at national level, as gaming patterns and social attitudes differ widely between countries. To protect the industry against money laundering, some jurisdictions limit the amount of cash that can be introduced and/or require reporting of such cash and/or require identification and monitoring of players. At an industry level, responsible gaming operators have also sought to protect the reputation of the industry by setting strict company and collective codes of behaviour.

Those planning to establish gaming operations need to take specialist advice in the jurisdiction in which they intend to be based and also any jurisdiction where they intend to operate. As with other businesses handling large sums, it is imperative to ensure staff are screened before they are employed and monitored once hired so as to prevent infiltration of the operation by launderers. In most jurisdictions where gambling is permitted operators will be required to perform client identification and reporting of large or unusual transactions, including betting with cash or with cash over a certain limit. As in other areas, seeking the help of a reputable industry association at an early stage is also highly advisable.

Some well-known indicators of suspicious activity include the:

- Purchase of gambling tokens for cash followed by a request to cash them in return for a cheque after minimal or clearly break even gaming activity
- Request for winnings to be paid by cheque to a third person
- Request for winnings to be credited to another (foreign) location of the same gaming chain
- Purchase of winning lottery tickets at a premium

In addition to gaming operators themselves, two other groups are at risk of involvement in money laundering in the gaming industry. Players need to be aware that the gaming operation that they patronise may not be honest. They may place bets with operations that are illegal or fraudulent. In both cases both stake money and any winnings may be at risk, not only of seizure by the authorities, but of simply disappearing – probably along with the operation concerned. They may face criminal charges of involvement if they cannot prove the legal origin of their stake money, which may prove easier said than done, and involve legal fees. Theft of identity, including credit card details may also occur.

There is also the more serious risk to *bona fide* professional advisers and suppliers of what are in fact illegal gaming operations of inadvertently facilitating money laundering, merely by providing services or goods in the normal course of business. Lawyers, accountants as well as marketing and advertising agents must be especially careful in this respect and perform enhanced CDD.

Remote Gaming

With advances in technology, instantaneous gaming across long distances with no face-to-face contact has become possible. Extending the banking analogy described above, unregulated remote gaming operations can be seen as unregulated offshore banking operations, providing similar degrees of anonymity to account holders through lax identification and poor audit trails.

Being technology driven, remote gaming via the internet and third generation mobile phones also offer the advantage of speed and 24 hour availability seven days a week. Such vulnerability to money laundering is in addition to an established vulnerability to fraud. According to a report by Mastercard in March 2002, Internet gaming already generates more than a fifth of all Internet fraud, making it the most serious of all Web-based crimes.

FATF Example 33: USD 178 million laundered through Internet gambling scheme

A joint investigation by the national criminal and fiscal police of Country C targeted a sports tout service (STC) providing gambling services by means of the Internet. The STC also functioned as an Internet service provider (ISP). The STC collected, collated and analysed statistical and other information relative to sporting events, and then sold this information to subscribers who would factor it into their betting decisions. The targeted STC/ISP expanded its services to include two offshore gambling operations located in the Caribbean region, both of which accepted wagers via the Internet or toll-free telephone numbers. Agents were successful in infiltrating the targeted operation.

To launder the proceeds from their illegal Internet gambling activities, the subjects of this investigation employed the services of a lawyer. He devised an elaborate scheme in which the STC/ISP leased its services to the subjects for a specified amount. Proceeds were also laundered through a series of bank accounts in the Caribbean area and eventually funnelled back to banking institutions in Country C. Investigators estimate that approximately USD 178 million was wagered through the STC/ISP annually.

It is anticipated that subjects in this investigation will be charged with gambling, money laundering, tax evasion and other organised crime related offences.

Following specific references to remote gaming in the Revised FATF 40 Recommendations, the possibility of using remote gaming operations for money laundering and terrorist financing has, somewhat belatedly, been recognised, as well as its other major attraction – scope for tax evasion.

With long distances and multiple jurisdictions possibly involved, the risk of involvement in illegal or unregulated, and thus potentially risky, gaming transactions are magnified. With no face-to-face contact, concerns about money laundering via remote gaming centre not so much on the placement of cash, but rather on the layering of funds.

This is principally undertaken by the transfer of winnings or returned deposits to parties other than the individual who originated the gaming transaction. It is not a hypothetical risk – in 2002 PayPal, the US online payments service, reached an agreement with New York State prosecutors to cease handling payments for local gaming operations, and in 2003 was cited by the US Attorney's Office for breaches of the US Patriot Act. It subsequently paid $10 million as part of a settlement agreement with the authorities

Operators need to establish with the relevant regulators that they are permitted in law to accept wagers from all jurisdictions in which the player may access the system. Players need to ensure their remote gaming partner is regulated in a reputable jurisdiction and a member of a *bona fide* industry association with a strict code of conduct, or they will run the same risks as with illegal "bricks and mortar" gaming operations.

Those offering services to gaming operations likewise need to guard against becoming involved in unwitting facilitation of money laundering at home or in a foreign jurisdiction. This can include ISPs and those arranging or carrying advertising for remote gaming operations such as banner or pop-up adverts on their websites.

FATF Example 34: Using a close resemblance to mask a laundering operation

The experience of the FIU from Country D shows that the following scheme is often used by criminals operating in that country:

An individual from Country D registers a gambling company "Gamblerz.com" in Country E where the name of the company is very similar to the name of a gambling company in Country F – "Gamblers.com" which operates legally and which has obtained a license. Thereafter, a website to promote the information on the game is set up in Country G in the name of "Gambler.com" which in turn is an abbreviation and common to both companies. Then an account is opened in Country H and thousands of people from Country J transfer their money to that account. The criminal can operate with the funds held in the said account with the help of a modem.

> The Individual withdraws USD 1 million by means of a modem from his account held with the bank. The activities are continued for several months but no license is obtained. As soon as the bank starts to query the transactions the individual who set up the operation (male) contacts the bank by telephone. Later another person (female) provides the documents requested by the bank; however, the documents do not seem to be genuine and marks of forgery can be detected.
>
> The bank freezes the account and reports to the FIU which takes the necessary steps in preparing materials for the police. Since it is it is a problem to determine in which country the crime has been committed, Country J opens a criminal case and launches criminal investigation to protect its own nationals who appear to be victims.

Guidance from the Interactive Gaming Council (IGC) advises reputable operators to establish tough client registration and ongoing verification processes in conjunction with the appropriate regulatory oversight and banking regulations. Ongoing "KYC" activity should be matched by use of smart technology to spot unusual patterns of gaming behaviour, report its occurrence and block any associated cash flows. As with regulation of financial businesses the other "Know Your" principles – business, employees, administration – are essential protection in the gaming industry. Likewise training plays a key role, both in raising awareness and helping to spot employees who may be the weak link in the chain.

High Value Goods

A fundamental objective of money laundering is the transformation of criminal proceeds into a less detectable form of asset. The fewer transactions required and the more liquid the asset involved, the more attractive that class of asset becomes for money launderers.

As a result, in addition to real estate (which is reviewed further on in this chapter), high value assets such as art and antiques, precious stones and metals, luxury cars, planes and boats have all attracted the attention of money launderers. Whilst subject in certain jurisdictions to import and export controls (which increases their scarcity value) works of art, gold and precious stones are relatively easy to smuggle internationally and can be valued within an acceptable degree of accuracy. They thus function readily as money substitutes.

As the following example shows, the purchase of a yacht in one jurisdiction and its sale or transfer in another was, for a long time, a relatively safe means of storing and transferring value. Regulatory interest, if any, was limited to the collection of any taxes arising. With the strengthening of anti-money laundering controls on the financial system in the 1990's it became clear that significant proceeds of crime were being redirected into high value goods, and regulation in this area has been tightened.

FATF Example 35: Cash laundered through purchases at auctions
A sophisticated criminal group importing cannabis resin into the country was arrested and approximately USD 2.5 million in assets were restrained. One method they used to launder their money was through cash purchases of large items at a public auction. The subjects purchased a house and boats, and the extent of the inquiry by the public auction regarding the source of the funds was satisfied by the suspect providing proof of a place of work.

FATF Recommendation 12 extends anti-money laundering procedures such as duty to have arrangements, training, CDD, record keeping and risk assessment to dealers in precious metals and precious stones. However, many jurisdictions have taken a much wider view and brought a broader range of high value goods dealers within the limits of national anti-money laundering legislation.

For example the EU 3rd Money Laundering Directive (which affects anti-money laundering legislation in 25 European countries) does not specify the type of high value goods dealer affected, but extends the directive to all dealers who accept the equivalent of Euro 15,000 or more in cash.

Depending on which countries you operate in you may be required to register or obtain a license before you are legally permitted to accept cash above a given limit. Registration or licensing may be accompanied by obligations to have more or less extensive anti-money laundering systems in place, backed up by an inspection and enforcement regime. Those intending to deal in high value goods, especially for cash, need to obtain advice from the relevant government departments, lawyers and sector associations in each jurisdiction of operation as to what it is they have to do in practice. Even where anti-money laundering measures are not a legal requirement, applying them will help to reduce the risk of abuse by money launderers.

Auctions

In many countries auctioneers are considered to be high value goods dealers. Auctions differ in a number of crucial ways from retail high value goods operations and these differences affect the application of anti-money laundering procedures and prudent business checks.

Client identification procedures need to be well thought out in advance for both buyers *and* sellers. This is important as auctions are fast moving affairs. Mistakes leading to failed sales may be hard to correct at the time of auction, and costly to correct thereafter.

Historically, auctions have often been cash based businesses, with large sums involved. Two or more successful bids (not uncommon for a car trader) *below* the cash threshold for client identification might easily form linked transactions *above* the threshold.

It is standard practice for auctioneers to accept commission bids and telephone bids to increase the bidding for lots. In the past such bidders have been looked on principally with a view to their creditworthiness. Legally, these clients may now constitute non face-to-face clients so measures to establish their identity and protect against possible money laundering may need to be enhanced.

There are a number of precautions that can be taken to protect against running foul of anti-money laundering legislation and/or money launderers when operating auctions. They include taking steps to:

- Require and specify documents to prove identity and/or residence
- Perform CDD, and not just on the immediate sellers of goods but also any third party you think they represent
- Perform CDD on purchasers making commission and telephone bids well in advance of the auction date, and reject late bidders applying to use this route
- (Where such rules apply) state in the auction documentation and advertising that those bidding in person who intend to pay in cash, in part or in whole, must provide full evidence of identity

"Genuine 24 carat. Never been used. Honest"

- Make it clear what form of payment is accepted, and specify acceptable alternatives to cash
- Pay net proceeds only to the sellers' bank accounts (not cash) and not to third party accounts
- Make it clear that suspicions will be reported
- Investigate unusual transactions, such as requests to sell assets with unrealistically low reserve prices, or repetitive patterns of sale.

The precise CDD rules will depend on your legal obligations and the degree of protection you are seeking against money launderers. The measures you take will depend on the risk profile of the transaction and parties involved. It is particularly important to identify successful bidders who wish to pay in cash where amounts exceed any threshold set by money laundering rules.

This includes multiple cash transactions below the threshold on the same day or over a period of time, and also applies when auctioneers bid on a client's behalf ("commission bids") and are to be paid in cash. It is usually not necessary to identify every other kind of attendee or bidder at an auction.

The Golden Rule in all cases is the same: if at any time you are unhappy about the nature of a seller's or buyer's true identity or purpose, you should decline to do business with them. It may be your legal duty so to do, and you may need to report your suspicions.

FATF Example 36: Diamond trading used as a cover for laundering of illicit funds

One of the files developed by the FIU of Country Y relates to a company with its registered office in an offshore centre, whose corporate object was especially broad and which, in particular, encompassed diamond trading. The account that this company held in Country Y formed the object of numerous international funds transfers in foreign currencies originating in a tax haven. The funds, in very large sums, were then systematically and immediately withdrawn in cash. These withdrawals were made in large denominations of foreign currencies by a third party, who was a director of companies active in diamond trading.

In view of the regularity of some of these operations, it was difficult to associate them with any legal commercial activity in the diamond sector, where one would expect the level of the funds generated to fluctuate. From information gathered by the FIU, it appeared that this account was used as a channelling account with the aim of hampering any investigations into the origin and ultimate destination of the funds.

Real Estate and Property Sector

There is a long history of links between property transactions and money laundering and the real estate sector has a number of features that make it attractive for money launderers. As a result, many countries now include estate agents (realtors) among the class of professional "gatekeepers" who are legally required to have anti-money laundering procedures.

The real estate and property market includes the housing and the commercial (including agricultural and industrial) sectors. A key feature of the second group is the greater likelihood that a transaction will involve higher values and cross-border components. Property transactions can be structured to create cash flows of widely differing location, size and timing, from small periodic local cash rental payments to very large one-off international electronic sale and purchase transfers.

Such transactions can be used to move funds and equally to provide a front for other money laundering activity. So too, property ownership is a common and perfectly legal activity, which lends an aura of respectability to those engaged in it. This helps money launderers gain the confidence of those they need to manipulate. Property is often attractive as a final stage in the money laundering cycle as it enables high concentration of assets.

FATF Example 37: Accountant and lawyers assist in a money laundering scheme

Suspicious flows of more than USD 2 million were identified being sent in small amounts by different individuals who ordered wire transfers and bank drafts on behalf of a drug trafficking syndicate who were importing 24 kg of heroin concealed in cargo into Country Z. Bank drafts purchased from different financial institutions in Country Y (the drug source country) were then used to purchase real estate in Country Z. An accountant was used by the syndicate to open bank accounts and register companies. The accountant also offered investment advice to the principals.

A firm of solicitors was also used by the syndicate to purchase the property using the bank drafts that had been purchased overseas after they had first been processed through the solicitors' trust account. Family trusts and companies were also set up by the solicitors

Real estate firms and individuals run the risk that they may be asked to advise on the sale and purchase or rental of property as well as its management and financing. There is thus more than one way in which they may encounter suspicious activity or become unwitting accomplices, the property sector now being subject to various degrees of regulation according to the jurisdiction involved. Such regulations may also apply to people who are not estate agents but who are involved professionally in the closing of real estate transactions, such as lawyers.

Property professionals engaged in arranging finance have for some time been subject to banking-style money laundering regulations in FATF compliant jurisdictions. More recently these countries have tightened controls, by requiring estate agents to establish basic anti-money laundering systems, and in certain countries, to register with a supervisory or enforcement agency. This is highly likely to be the cases if the estate agent accepts cash from, or on behalf of, a client, whether for the full amount of the transaction or the deposit.

FATF Example 38: Use of mortgages and property

A lawyer was instructed by his client, a drug trafficker, to deposit cash into the lawyer's trust account and then make routine payments for mortgages on properties beneficially owned by the drug trafficker. The lawyer received commissions from the sale of these properties and brokering the mortgages. While he later admitted to receiving the cash from the trafficker, depositing same into his trust account, and administering payments to the trafficker's mortgages, he denied knowledge of the source of the funds.

It is important for real estate agents to know the law as it applies to the country or countries in which they operate. As with other sectors it is important to look at how key terms are defined. The law will most likely require client identification (possibly on both sides of a transaction), suspicious activity reporting and record keeping, as well as supporting systems and training. In certain jurisdictions such as the US, such arrangements will need to be audited.

The examples above of money laundering schemes involving property illustrate points to watch. Some other Red Flags include:

- Client spontaneously offers to pay generous commission/fees
- Frequent changes to instructions on handling of rental payments
- Transaction inconsistent with client's apparent means, occupation or purpose.

Estate agents can offer a wide range of services including, for example, investment and mortgage advice, and rent collection involving cash. It is therefore important for them to be aware which particular part of anti-money laundering regulations apply to the business they are undertaking and the regime for any non-standard special tasks they may be requested to perform.

Accountancy and related Professions

A wide range of professionals operates in the accountancy sector. Broadly speaking they fall into two main categories, those who are employees of a given business, such as bookkeepers, accountants and auditors in finance and internal control departments, and those who have a client relationship with businesses, such as external auditors and liquidators.

Whether internal or external, accountants and allied professions play a central role in a client's operations across the whole business life cycle. Whilst they cannot know everything that goes on in a client's operations, by the very nature of their work, accountancy professionals are often strategically placed when it comes to preventing money laundering.

Accountants provide advice and services connected with company formation and management, design accounting systems, process and report on transactions as well as providing tax planning and auditing services. At the far end of the business cycle, accountants advise on the disposal of a company through sale, flotation and mergers, or, if the business is failing, on insolvency issues. Accountants also offer specialist services such as investment advice, forensic accounting, IT systems development, risk analysis and systems audit.

All businesses need to record their affairs in a way that allow owners and regulatory authorities to follow an audit trail of company income and expenditure. Accountants help establish the form and content of these records and design the controls and reporting systems that go with them. They often supervise or check that such systems work as they should. This natural access to company financial records is matched by few other employees and professionals, again meaning that accountants may have insight into potential threats.

For the same reasons, accountants are also especially at risk from coming into contact with money launderers. External accountants can be targeted by money launderers and asked to undertake transactions involving the opening of bank accounts. An internal or external accountant may be asked to design systems, which are then abused to launder money. Accountants may also see their *bona fide* client being tricked into a laundering money scam, or simply stumble across unwitting suspect activity in the course of their work.

Given their role and vulnerability, accountants have legal and professional duties to report suspicions of money laundering. These apply whether they are internal or externally employed and in some cases even cover well-founded suspicions formed incidentally during the course of their work. If they are business owners or directors, accountants may have an enhanced duty of care because of their professional status.

FATF Example 39: Laundering operation is set up by accounting firm

In March 2000, the Director of an insurance company from a country in Asia (Country C) defrauded the company of USD 90 million by purporting to have purchased bonds of the same amount. The proceeds were paid through two companies registered in a Caribbean island country (Country D) and holding bank accounts in another Asian country (Country E). The Country D companies and the bank accounts had been set up and run by an Asian accounting firm for the offending Director. The USD 90 million was firstly paid to one of the Country D companies, then transferred to the other, and then back to Country C to a third company also owned by the Director, all in the same day. The Director has since been arrested by the Country C Police and is in custody pending trial.

The accounting firm failed to note the U-turn movement of the funds as suspicious and thus did not make any disclosure. Moreover, in September 2000, staff of the accounting firm became aware of the Director's fraud and that he had used the Country D companies and accounts set up by their firm to launder the funds. Still the management committee of the accounting firm did not make any disclosure to the authorities. They limited their action to ascertaining if they could be liable in any way for negligence. The four-member management committee of the accounting firm (all senior accounting firm partners) and the partner who handled the account have all been arrested for an offence of failing to make a disclosure.

Governments have been quick to spot the risk of accountants being targeted by money launderers seeking gateways to the financial system. Governments also target accountants not just as gatekeepers but as watchdogs, who can check and report on the adequacy of anti-money laundering measures in other firms. Forensic accountants are also increasingly used by governments to investigate cases of money laundering and financial transactions relating to precursor offences.

Internal and external accountants must therefore be aware of anti-money laundering legislation as well as local and international professional standards that apply to them and their firm. If they are external accountants they also need to know the law and standards as they apply in the client context. But above all accountants must be very careful to protect themselves against unwitting involvement in money laundering schemes.

FATF Example 40: Failure to disclose suspicious activity by financial professional

In a recent major loan sharking investigation in an Asian country, an accountant responsible for auditing the accounts of a company, which had received crime proceeds laundered through a neighbouring State, failed to report any suspicious transactions. Investigators found obvious discrepancies in the company's account records which should have alerted the accountant, such as unexplained large-summed payments from and to the Director (who was the mastermind of the loan sharking syndicate), the fact that no delivery or warehousing expenses were ever booked for the trades purportedly conducted, and that in one instance the date of delivery of the "goods" to the buyer actually predated the date of acquisition by the seller. The accountant, when questioned, stated that he failed to note any suspicion because he only looked at the year-end figures for the purposes of certification of the accounts.

The principles of self-help involved are the same as with other regulated business sectors. Accountants must perform careful client identification checks and develop effective risk-based systems to cover both client acceptance procedures and the identification of suspicious transactions. Those acting internationally are well advised to pay special attention to subtle variations in key high level legal definitions (such as "accountancy", "reasonable explanation" "knowledge", "suspicion", "unusual") which may trap the unwary. Like other sectors, they must establish appropriate training and reporting systems, including appointing a MLRO, set up record keeping systems to preserve key documents, and avoid tipping off.

This latter point highlights the conflicts between contractual and fiduciary duties on the one hand and legal obligations on the other, and indeed the conflicts between competing legal obligations. Thus reporting to client management the suspicion of money laundering may inadvertently lead to tipping off, as it may neither be possible to tell who is involved nor to control the use of information divulged to management. In this case a report should be made direct to a proper authority in the public interest without delay and without informing the client.

Note also that where an accountant is handling client monies, which may actually belong to a third party, in some jurisdictions the accountant may risk becoming a constructive trustee of those funds. This may create a conflict between following client instructions and protecting the interests of the rightful owner.

Given the prevalence of crime, and thus money laundering, it is highly likely that accountancy professionals will discover money laundering at some stage in their career. It is also likely that accountants will become unwittingly involved in some capacity in establishing or running anti-money laundering arrangements, especially highly complex or subtle ones, if they do not exercise due caution.

Most high net worth individuals take steps to avoid (as opposed to evade) tax, as do many corporates. Avoidance is legal, but evasion is illegal and one of the more common problems for accountants is suspicion of tax evasion. A firm's anti money-laundering measures may, for example, highlight the use of offshore structures to warehouse income and gains and structures used to transfer funds. In marginal situations, it is hard to differentiate between legal tax avoidance schemes and illegal tax evasion schemes which by definition give rise to money laundering offences. Accountants must be alert to such situations.

It must be stressed that any such discovery or involvement may not be immediately apparent to the accountant at the time. Money laundering has its own patterns, which may only be revealed over time and which are unlikely to be caught by controls designed for other purposes such as management or statutory reporting or fraud prevention. Indeed, money laundering schemes are often designed specifically to work around such controls.

To help detect potential money laundering the international accountancy body IFAC has produced a set of Red Flags for accountants, which are reflected in Appendix 4. For best effect these should be used in the context of a full control environment, with proper risk assessment, controls, reporting and monitoring. Various national professional bodies as well as IFAC provide guidance on what this involves. Appendix 2 contains a link to the IFAC website from which the latest edition of the IFAC anti-money laundering guide can be downloaded.

Lawyers And Paralegals

Lawyers are in a similar position to accountants and other professionals in that they offer services to help firms and individuals to manage their affairs. If money launderers wish to operate behind the cover of an apparently legitimate business, then they must create a business (such as a private company or a trust) at least in form. The ability to abuse lawyers' skills has great value, the more so if they are part of a prestigious firm unwittingly or recklessly providing services.

FATF Example 41: Failure to disclose suspicious activity by legal professional

A firm of lawyers was asked by a client to assist in the arrangement of a substantial loan to a third party. The solicitor tasked with assisting the client was instructed to request some form of guarantee from the third party. The third party initially sent an insurance bond, which turned out on inspection to be worthless. The lawyer requested another guarantee and received share certificates in a foreign company; however, these proved to have been stolen. The lawyer made a third request and received some prime bank guarantees with a value far in excess of the initial loan. The lawyer was then asked by the first client to assist in the sale of the prime bank guarantees by certifying as to their authenticity, which he proceeded to do using letterhead stationery from the law firm. Despite the suspicious circumstances, the lawyer made no disclosure to law enforcement and, at the time of writing, left his firm potentially exposed due to his willingness to "certify" documents often known to be used in international frauds.

Law firms are also gateways to the financial system through their provision of client accounts, and by their acting as agents. They can also advise on the best way to structure business interests from a tax or regulatory standpoint; the transfer of real estate property is another important aspect of their work. All these areas are common vectors of money laundering, and carry varying degrees of risk.

Whether a sole practitioner, a member of a firm or member of an in-house legal team, lawyers are under a professional as well as a legal duty to help prevent money laundering. The higher degree of knowledge lawyers possess may also heighten the level of care they must demonstrate in observing anti-money laundering requirements.

In some jurisdictions, however, the legal profession has historically made relatively few useful suspicious activity reports compared to the banking sector. Moreover, people with legal knowledge can sometimes be induced to adopt a criminal course, meaning that law firms and third party businesses must be aware that legal qualifications alone do not make for an honest individual – KYE still applies.

FATF Example 42: Lawyer assists in setting up a complex laundering scheme

This case involved 19 individuals in the medical service industry, one being both a lawyer and an accountant. This dossier submitted for prosecution contained 123 violations involving conspiracy, false claims, wire fraud and money laundering. The false claims involved fictitious patient claims and claims for services which were not provided.

The two primary subjects employed the lawyer's services to set up four interrelated shell corporations as the controlling entities. In addition, eight nominee corporations were created to generate fictitious health care service records reflecting in-home therapy and nursing care. Health care providers including therapists, registered nurses and physicians operated the nominee corporations. To keep the health care billing, tax return filings and bank account records synchronised, the two main subjects relied on the lawyer/ accountant defendant.

In excess of USD 4 million was laundered through bank accounts in cities of the north and south-east of the country and through suspected offshore accounts. Numerous accounts were created at four or five separate banks for purposes of amassing and moving these funds. Cashier's cheques often were purchased and even negotiated through the lawyer/accountant's trust account for concealment of property acquisition. This defendant was sentenced to two years in exchange for his co-operation.

Both primary defendants were ordered to forfeit real and personal property, including the USD 4 million and purchased property. They received five- and two-year prison sentences respectively. Two additional related case defendants (one being an elected official), laundered an additional USD 2 million and were charged with 33 violations of the law in a separate case. They were ordered to forfeit USD 95,000 in currency. The former elected official received a five-year prison sentence.

In addition to the risk of being tricked into providing or procuring channels for illegitimate funds, law firms also risk being used as "stalking horses". This is when criminals ask apparently innocuous questions or request a particular service to gain information on how to avoid anti-money laundering procedures. It is important to be on guard against this form of threat, which can have legal and reputational repercussions.

Understanding the law and any national professional guidelines is the first step in self-protection. Thereafter the same basic principles apply. Firms are required to have suitable anti-money laundering arrangements, covering the usual functions of client identification, training, record keeping and reporting. An MLRO, sometimes called a nominated officer, must be appointed to handle SARs.

Importantly, legislation may apply to all staff in a law firm and not just those with legal qualifications – for example those handling client account monies. Such arrangements are usually set up using a risk-based approach. In essence this means that the more a person has client contact, access to sensitive data, or authority to execute legal documents or financial transactions, the more attention must be paid to possible money laundering risks arising from their activities. However, some practice areas are inherently less at risk from money laundering than others, and require reduced compliance measures.

Legislation generally takes care to preserve legal privilege; however there are issues as to the compatibility of monitoring client business for potentially suspicious events and reporting obligations. Lawyers are not generally required to report suspicious activity if the relevant information is subject to legal professional privilege. Where privilege starts and ends has always been grey area, and requires specialist consideration of the particular circumstances.

It may be that a client's motives and actions appear innocuous interpreted one way, but suspicious when interpreted another. There may come a point where a lawyer feels he or she is no longer in the realms of advising the client on, for example, a matter of tax law, but is defending him or herself against a possible charge of assisting in tax evasion.

Lawyers must be careful what advice they give to their client and what advice they take themselves. Where concern becomes reasonable suspicion then the question of terminating the retainer and what to do next must be given immediate consideration.

Company And Trust Formation Agents And Service Providers

The stock in trade of this sector is the perfectly legal user-friendly establishment and management of entities that can accept, hold and dispose of assets on an international basis. Services include:

- Setting up entities on behalf of clients
- Acting as officers, trustees, principals and nominee shareholders
- Providing or arranging registered and accommodation addresses.

Fair Exchange

The company and trust services area is generally considered to be at high risk of abuse by money launderers, and in many jurisdictions the sector is subject to regulation. The primary concern is the misuse of facilities established by the sector, rather than the corruption of professionals themselves, though this does present problems from time to time.

FATF Example 43: A trust is used for laundering the proceed of alcohol smuggling

Some years ago a national of Country A was convicted of smuggling a huge quantity of alcohol. Just a small part of the proceeds were confiscated. The police found documents showing that his companies in Country A had mortgage loans from a company owned by a trust from a small island jurisdiction (Country B). After the conviction, the FIU in Country A learned that it was the convicted person and later his common law wife who were the beneficial owners of the company. With assistance from the office of the public prosecutor in Country B, the FIU got information which showed that the company received money from a bank account in a third country (Country C). It was suspected that the proceeds from the smuggling had been transported as cash to the Country C bank, then to the trust in Country B and finally back to Country A as "mortgage loans". It was clear that neither the companies nor the convicted person or his common law wife had paid any instalments.

Whilst core players in the company formation sector maintain strict standards, in some countries low barriers to entry and ineffective national associations allow marginal players to gain a foothold. There is also the problem that certain governments which operate direct company formation systems do not perform the same controls as they demand of service providers.

The steady number of cases involving shady operators in this sector suggests that, despite tighter controls and penalties, the inducements to help money launderers structure schemes remain attractive.

Money launderers misuse the sector especially in the layering process. They exploit the fact that some jurisdictions have laws allowing ownership and control of companies and trusts to remain secret. Even where this is not the case, assets can be moved quickly through multiple companies and trusts in various countries, creating a tangled web of legal obstacles to asset tracing. As already seen, this is sometimes known as drawing the "corporate veil" over criminal reality.

FATF Example 44: A lawyer uses offshore companies and trust accounts to launder money

Mr. S headed an organisation importing narcotics into country A, from country B. A lawyer was employed by Mr. S to launder the proceeds of this operation.

To launder the proceeds of the narcotics importing operation, the lawyer established a web of offshore corporate entities. These entities were incorporated in a Country C, where scrutiny of ownership, records, and finances was not strong. A local management company in Country D administered these companies. These entities were used to camouflage movement of illicit funds, acquisition of assets, and financing criminal activities. Mr. S was the holder of 100% of the bearer share capital of these offshore entities.

In Country A, a distinct group of persons and companies without any apparent association to Mr. S transferred large amounts of money to Country D where it was deposited in, or transited through Mr. S's offshore companies. This same web network was found to have been used to transfer large amounts of money to a person in Country E who was later found to be responsible for drug shipments destined for Country A;

Several other lawyers and their trust accounts were used to receive cash and transfer funds, ostensibly for the benefit of commercial clients in Country A. When they were approached by law enforcement during the investigation, many of these lawyers cited "privilege" in their refusal to co-operate. Concurrently, the lawyer established a separate similar network (which included other lawyers' trust accounts) to purchase assets and place funds in vehicles and instruments designed to mask the beneficial owner's identity. The lawyer has not been convicted of any crime in Country A. Investigators allege however that his connection to and actions on behalf of Mr. S are irrefutable.

Trusts and companies also allow money launderers to maintain arms length control of funds, for example by giving friends, relatives and trusted advisers powers to administer funds at their discretion, or by naming them as a beneficiary.

Agents and service providers must keep an eye on four main risks:

- Have they identified the ultimate beneficial owner of the structures they are being asked to create?
- Are they being used by money launderers?
- Are their clients being used by money launderers?
- Are they observing third party money laundering transactions in the course of their work?

Because of the high risk factor, firms in this sector are coming under tighter regulation. The importance of anti-money laundering arrangements in this sector, especially CDD, cannot be overemphasised, both with regard to client identification, transaction monitoring and, above all, establishing the beneficial ownership of the structures being created.

Likewise it is important to establish clearly that staff employed by company formation agencies are who they say they are, and not criminals attempting to obtain covert access to the services on offer. The rule of identify or abandon the relationship applies here as well.

In addition to the KYC Red Flags in Appendix 4, other points to watch are offers of enhanced fees, for example under the guise of wanting to get matters settled quickly, and inquiries with reference to bearer shares or warrants. As many company formations (not just those offshore) are done at a distance, identification may be complicated by conflicts over which set or sets of anti-money laundering regulations apply to the formation. Legal advice may be needed.

Charities

Historically speaking there is a long tradition of links between charities (also called not-for-profit organisations or NFPOs) and money laundering. But modern threats are not limited to phoney appeals or disguising drug proceeds as donations to schools in South America.

Political extremists used charities extensively in the late 20th Century and, with the upturn in high profile attacks since then, policy makers and law enforcement agencies have been paying renewed attention to the link between NFPOs and the funding of terrorism linked to religious fundamentalism. The UN and individual nations have published special lists of organisations and individuals believed to be involved in terrorism. It is often a strict liability offence to act for a party on these lists.

Charities have always been attractive to terrorist organisations for a number of reasons:

- A cultural, religious or sporting charity provides respectable cover for the establishment and operations of an organisation, whose objectives may be far from culture, religion or sport as they are generally understood
- They are relatively easy to set up, with few or no checks of incorporation or operations. This is especially the case where:
- there is constitutional protection of the rights of assembly and free speech
- NFPOs usually have bank accounts and can deposit cash without raising immediate suspicions. They have *bona fide* reasons for distributing money to countries world wide, especially those in or near conflict zones.

NFPOs can be subverted by terrorist organisations unknown to many of those associated with them for example by key staff or trustees taking over operations, changing objectives and diverting funds. Charities can also be established to target particular sections of

Pro bono…

society in or across countries and where it is commonly known that the "charity" is a political or fighting fund. In either case the net result is that terrorists can collect, move and apply funds with only small risk of detection.

FATF Example 45: Misuse of a position within an NPO and unwitting donors

Non-profit organisation P had branch offices in different countries where it had co-operative development projects. Individuals associated with a terrorist organisation ran some of these branches. Organisation P was however unaware that key persons working in its offices in Country X had connections with this terrorist organisation.

Organisation P had a headquarters in Country X, and one of its offices was located in a beneficiary country (Country Y). Despite the fact that Mr. B, the person in charge of Organisation P in Country Y, was not included in the employees' roll in Country X, he nevertheless received donations from different people and international bodies. Mr. B diverted those funds to a terrorist organisation, taking advantage of his position and anonymity in Country X.

This activity was made easier because the project was financed by donors who were unaware of the total amount of money involved. It was therefore possible to maintain an unjustified amount of money. In addition, since the projects were carried out in very remote areas, there was some delay before the beneficiaries discovered that they had only received a small amount of money. The investigation was difficult because the donors were also responsible for verifying the carrying out of the project. In this case, because the donors were certain public sector organisations, the checks were never performed.

Those dealing with NFPOs as donors, service providers or business partners need to be sure that the charity they are dealing with is not intending to abuse its position and is not being abused by third parties. Failure to establish these two points may lead to unwitting involvement in the funding of terrorism, a crime that carries penalties as severe as those for committing an act of terrorism itself. It is important to know the full picture and what other donors are involved.

FATF Example 46 : NPO used as a cover for an IMVT service

The financial supervisory authority (FSA) of Country D has detected an increasing tendency for underground banking businesses with world-wide operating networks to try to circumvent the obligation to obtain a license by establishing themselves an incorporated association to serve as a cover for their illegal business of remittance services.

In several cases Country D's FSA shut down unauthorised remittance businesses. Later, however, the FSA found out that the same persons continued the business but had established and registered as associations for charitable purposes and hoped somehow to have placed their illegal business out of reach of the FSA. One typical example is the case of Association L for help in an African country (Country K) and with its headquarters in Country D. It is part of an obviously worldwide operating network including for example offices in Europe, North America, the Pacific region and the Middle East.

The pattern used is the same in all of the known cases as for the Association L case: The Country D branch of this association collected money from its principals and promised them to transfer and disburse the money to specified beneficiaries especially in Country K. Since its registration in mid-January 2002 until July 2002 Association A transferred approximately USD 500,000 before the office was closed down again.

There are some straightforward steps you can take to protect yourself from such risks.

- If you are asked as an adviser in a regulated service or industry to assist a NFPO in a professional capacity, you should perform full client ID, *even if you are undertaking the work on a "pro bono" basis.* Do not omit checks that you would normally undertake for a paying client
- Check that the organisation or its key individuals are not on a list of suspects. This may be difficult where foreign names have to be translated into your own language and you may need to take advice
- Check that the organisation is in good standing with the tax authorities. If the charity operates in more than one jurisdiction you may need to establish its status on a broad basis. These checks should be independent and not in the form of a certificate from the organisation itself.
- Use common sense to judge whether the NFPO acts in a manner that is consistent with its size and resources. Is a small charity only

The ring of confidence tricksters

using local collection boxes moving huge sums? Is it suddenly active after a long period of stagnation? Has it suddenly gone quiet?

- Be on the lookout for approaches by different NFPOs which share the same address, management, objectives, funding base or which all direct funds or inquiries to the same bank or professional adviser
- Ask around, including other reputable charities operating in the same sector. This can be by means of a direct question or asking them to name the genuine NFPOs operating in a given sector

- Pay particular attention to transactions, organisations and people associated with high-risk jurisdictions.

These checks are in addition to the normal precautions you should take if you see unusual transactions and begin to form suspicions.

NOTES:
1. An arrangement with a bank in another country enabling payments to be made and received easily and transferred onwards as required.
2. For an example, see Regulation 4(3)(6) of the UK Money Laundering Regulations 2003.
3. The term "hawala" comes from the Arabic meaning to "change" or "transform." It is used also to refer to a bill of exchange or promissory note and a wire or electronic funds transfer. The allied expression "hawala safar" means " traveller's cheque".
4. Finance & Development Dec 2002 (IMF)

APPENDICES

Types of Business usually covered by Money Laundering Regulations

A. Financial Institutions

"Financial Institutions" means any person or entity who conducts as a business one or more of the following activities or operations for or on behalf of a customer:

1. Acceptance of deposits and other repayable funds from the public[1]
2. Lending[2]
3. Financial leasing[3]
4. The transfer of money or value[4]
5. Issuing and managing means of payment (e.g. credit and debit cards, cheques, traveller's cheques, money orders and banker's drafts, electronic money)
6. Financial guarantees and commitments
7. Trading in:
   (a) money market instruments (cheques, bills, CDs, derivatives etc.)
   (b) Foreign exchange
   (c) Exchange, interest rate and index instruments
   (d) Transferable securities
   (e) Commodity futures trading
8. Participation in securities issues and the provision of financial services related to such issues
9. Individual and collective portfolio management

10. Safekeeping and administration of cash or liquid securities on behalf of other persons
11. Otherwise investing, administering or managing funds or money on behalf of other persons
12. Underwriting and placement of life insurance and other investment related insurance[5]
13. Money and currency changing

B. Designated non-financial businesses and professions

"Designated non-financial businesses and professions" means:

(a) Casinos
(b) Real Estate Agents
(c) Dealers in precious metals
(d) Dealers in precious Stones
(e) Lawyers, notaries other independent legal professionals and accountants – this refers to sole practitioners, partners or employed professionals within professional firms[6]. It is not meant to refer to 'internal' or 'in house' professionals that are employees of other types of businesses, nor to professionals working for government agencies, who may already be subject to measures to combat money laundering
(f) Trust and Company Service Providers – this refers to all persons or businesses that are not covered elsewhere, and which as a business provide any of the following services to third parties:

- acting as a formation agent of legal persons
- acting as (or arranging for another person to act as) a director or secretary of a company, a partner or a partnership, or a similar position in relation to other legal persons
- providing a registered office, business address or accommodation, correspondence or administrative address for a company, a partnership or any other legal person or arrangement
- acting as (or arranging for another person to act as) a trustee of an express trust

• acting as (or arranging for another person to act as) a nominee shareholder for another person.

APPENDIX 2.

Sources of Help and Information

ICC – CCS
ICC Commercial Crime Services
Maritime House, 1 Linton Road
Barking, Essex IG11 8HG, United Kingdom
Tel + 44 (0)20 8591 3000
Fax + 44 (0)20 8594 2833
E-mail ccs@icc-ccs.org
http://www.icc-ccs.org.uk/

A. International Institutions
Bank for International Settlements (BIS)
http://www.bis.org/bcbs/publ_13.htm
European Union (EU)
http://europa.eu.int/comm/internal_market/company/financial-crime/index_en.htm#moneylaundering
International Monetary Fund (IMF)
http://www.imf.org/external/np/exr/facts/aml.htm
Organisation for Economic Co-operation and Development (OECD)
http://www1.oecd.org/daf/nocorruptionweb/moneylaundering/index.htm
Organisation of American States
http://www.cicad.oas.org/Lavado_Activos/ENG/About.asp#

World Bank

http://web.worldbank.org/WBSITE/EXTERNAL/WBI/WBIPROGRA
MS/PSGLP/0,,contentMDK:20292990~menuPK:461615~pagePK:6415615
8~piPK:64152884~theSitePK:461606,00.html

United Nations

www.imolin.org/imolin/en/uninstruments.html

B. International Standard Setting, Regulatory and Supervisory Groupings

FATF

FATF – *Financial Action Task Force*

http://www.fatf-gafi.org

Forty Recommendations (2003)

http://www.fatf-gafi.org/dataoecd/7/40/34849567.PDF

Special Recommendations on Terrorist Financing (2001)

Interpretative Notes

*http://www.fatf-
gafi.org/document/9/0,2340,en_32250379_32236920_34032073_1_1_1_1,0
0.html*

FATF-Style Regional Bodies

APGML – Asia Pacific Group on Money Laundering

http://www.apgml.org

CFATF – Caribbean Financial Action Task Force

http://www.cfatf.org

EAG – Eurasian Group

http://www.euroasiangroup.org/

ESAAMLG – Eastern and Southern Africa Anti-Money Laundering Group

http://www.esaamlg.org/

GAFISUD – Financial Action Task Force on Money Laundering in South
America

http://www.sepblac.es/ingles/acerca_sepblac/gafisud.thm

MONEYVAL – Council of Europe Select Committee of Experts on the
Evaluation of Anti-Money Laundering Measures
(formerly PC-R-EV)

148

http://www.coe.int/T/E/Legal_affairs/Legal_co-
operation/Combating_economic_crime/Money_laundering/
MENAFATF – Middle East and North Africa FATF
http://www.menafatf.org/home.asp

Sector Bodies
Basel Committee on Banking Supervision (BCBS)
http://www.bis.org/publ/bcbs.htm
Financial Stability Forum
*http://*www.fsforum.org
International Accounting Standards Board (IASB)
http://www.iasb.org
International Association of Insurance Supervisors (IAIS)
http://www.iaisweb.org
International Federation of Accounting Bodies (IFAC)
http://www.ifac.org
International Organisation of Securities Commissions (IOSCO)
http://www.iosco.org/library/pubdocs
International Bar Association (IBA)
http://www.anti-moneylaundering.org/
Offshore Group of Banking Supervisors
http://www.ogbs.net/

C. Information on Countries, Organisations and Individuals
FATF NCCT list
http://www.fatf-
gafi.org/document/4/0,2340,en_32250379_32236992_33916420_1_1_1_1,0
0.html
UN lists
http://www.un.org/Docs/sc/committees/1267/tablelist.htm
OFAC
http://www.treas.gov/offices/enforcement/ofac/sdn/
Experian
http://www.experian.com

D&B
http://www.dnb.com
INTERPOL
http://www.interpol.int
OECD List of Tax Havens
http://www.oecd.org
Transparency International
*http://*www.ti.org

D. Information on Money Laundering Threats and Typologies

FATF Report on Money Laundering Typologies (1997 –2005)
http://www.fatf-gafi.org
US Treasury FinCEN
http://www.fincen.gov

All web addresses as at date of publication.

APPENDIX 3.

Types of Document and Data providing Evidence of Identity

Natural Persons
Natural persons are normally identified by a combination of primary and secondary documents. Some documents are placed in different categories in different countries according to the robustness of issuing procedures. The following division reflects common practice:

Primary Documents
Primary documents are typically issued by a central or regional government department and provide a combination of the following identifiers:

- Surname, given names and married name (if any)
- Mother's maiden (birth) name
- Usual or registered address
- Place and/or date of birth
- Nationality
- Type of, and unique number assigned to, the primary document
- Unique number assigned to the individual
- Issuing authority, place of issue and date
- Expiry date
- Photograph and/or biometric identifier
- Signature

Primary documents that contain all or some of this information include:

- National identity card
- Residents permit
- Passport
- Certificate of citizenship
- Record of landing
- Driving licence
- Official birth certificate extract
- Extract from official register of residents
- Work permit
- Naturalisation certificate
- Armed forces identity card
- Diplomatic identity card
- Firearms licence

Secondary Documents

Secondary documents are typically issued by a public or private sector bodies. They do not provide proof of identity in themselves but corroborate and extend information obtained from primary documents, e.g. by providing recent address details. They usually contain the following information:

- Name of employer
- Name of utility or service provider
- Health insurance and/or doctor's details
- Social security number
- Address

Secondary documents include:

- Workplace identity card
- Student identity card
- Utility bill
- Season ticket or senior citizen travel pass
- National or private healthcare system registration card
- Social security card
- Pension book
- Correspondence with fiscal authorities
- Identity cards issued by local diplomatic missions.
- Voter registration card
- Rates or tax bill
- Bank statement
- Tenancy agreement

The following documents can be useful with establishing names:

- Marriage certificates
- Adoption certificates
- Divorce certificates

Legal Persons

Legal persons are normally identified by a combination of documents according to the law of the relevant country, e.g.:

- Certificate of incorporation
- Copy of court registration
- Extract from the register of companies

- Copy of application for registration
- Articles of association
- List of principals and secretary
- List of authorised signatories
- Copies of powers of attorney issued
- Tax registration certificates
- Members' register

These documents should contain:

- Name and abbreviated name
- Address of registered office
- Address of local branch office (foreign enterprises)

"Does two villains beat three of a dodgy kind?"

- Principal/permitted activities
- Number of identification document,
- Name and position of authorised representatives
- Identification data of agent for service of process

Authorised officers, signatories and agents are identified as per natural persons.

APPENDIX 4.

"Red Flags"

Use of Cash

- Payments with small denomination notes, uncommonly wrapped, with postal orders or similar
- Frequent or large deposits of currency and dealing only in cash equivalents
- Asking for exemptions from regulations on deposit of cash and cash equivalents
- Small amounts (with possible large totals) are collected from sources unconnected with the business, then passed on by Electronic Funds Transfer (EFT)
- Use of notes in a size unusual for the nature of business
- Frequent changing of small notes for larger ones
- Unusual markings on notes or other bills
- Repeated use of automated cash deposit machines/purchase of travellers cheques for sums just below threshold
- Repeated cash transfers to or from foreign banks or companies
- Invoices settled by cash or transfer by unrelated companies
  Repeated cash receipts or payments by a customer who normally makes or receives transfers by cheque or bank giro
- Sudden imbalance between cash and non-cash deposits/withdrawals

KYB

- Ignorance of how own business or relevant business sector operates
- Transactions lack business sense, a clear strategy or are inconsistent with the customer's objectives
- Trading with little or no risk
- Churning (excessive journal entries between accounts without any apparent business purpose)
- High turnover of funds but no apparent substantive business
- Indifference to high risk and high transaction costs
- Dealing high risk securities (legitimate but associated with fraud)
- Dealings with high risk areas without clear rationale
- Repeat transactions for amounts just under the reporting limit
- Frequent EFT receipt with balance drawn down by cheque or debit card without any apparent business purpose
- Sudden large payment to or from abroad without apparent reason
- Transfers to unrelated third parties
- Deposit of a large sum for a stated purpose where the amount is suddenly paid away for different ends or with no explanation.
- Unduly complex arrangements
- Inconsistencies in an account's activities such as size, destination and timing of payments, especially international transfers
- Inconsistency of business with businesses of similar size in the same industry.
  Personal and firm funds are intermingled
- Pressure exerted to avoid record keeping or reporting requirements
- Requests to process transactions in such a manner to avoid the firm's normal documentation requirements

KYC

- Name of past client is used as an introduction but the former client has now a new address or is uncontactable
- Company address is that of a service company or agent
- Identity documents are from non-native countries especially less

well known countries, or are diplomatic passports, or are photocopies (with our without excuse)

- Unreadiness, unwillingness or inability to provide information and/or verifiable documentation about self, business organisation, key officials, owners or controllers, business plans
- Provision of no or false or misleading statements about origins of funds especially after specific request
- Customer shows unusual interest in the firm's compliance with anti-money laundering policies and SAR procedures when discussing identity, type of business and source of assets
- Negative background checks on customer and known associates
- Evasiveness about links to a suspected principal
- Unusual or suspicious identification or business documents
- Business is alleged to be part of a confidential venture involving a blue chip organization, a government body, or well known high net worth individual
- The business is going to support good works in general or a particular charity
- Opening of multiple accounts with similar names
- Inconsistency of information provided with itself or other information obtained, usual business practices, appearance and behaviour of client
- The business is run by someone who has inside knowledge of a highly lucrative market

Insurance Red Flags

- Request for an unsuitable product with no adequate reason
- More interest in the cancellation or surrender terms than in the return
- Request to upsize small policies or transactions based on regular payments by means of a large lump payment
- Acceptance of unfavourable terms in relation to health or age.
- Contract for life insurance of below three years
- Request come through unknown broker or broker in region with light regulation

- The first (or single) premium is paid from a bank account overseas, especially lightly regulated countries
- Purchase of insurance products using a third party cheque
- Use of a performance bond resulting in a cross border payment
- Frequent changes to beneficiaries
- Attempt to borrow maximum cash value of a single premium policy soon after purchase
- Client cancels investment or insurance soon after purchase, especially where reimbursement is requested to a third party.

NOTES:

1. This also captures private banking
2. This includes inter alia: consumer credit; mortgage credit; factoring, with or without recourse; and finance of commercial transaction (including forfeiting)
3. This does not extend to financial leasing arrangements in relation to consumer products
4. This applies to financial activity in both the formal or informal sector, e.g. alternative remittance activity. See the Interpretative Note to Special Recommendation VI. It does not apply to any natural or legal person who provides financial institutions solely with message or other support systems for transmitting funds. See the Interpretative Note to Special Recommendation VII.
5. Applies both to insurance undertakings and insurance intermediaries (agents and brokers).
6. Includes lawyers conducting real estate, corporate and financial transactions but generally excludes litigation advice.

INDEX